What Board Me
Bec

"Brilliant! I just started reading this book, but it's utterly captivating and deeply insightful. The real-life examples from Beverly's 25+ years of experience performing board evaluations around the world is worth the price of admission alone! A must-read for anyone looking to 'up their game' in the boardroom."
– **Christine Carter, Fellow of the Chartered Governance Institute**

"An outstanding book! I ordered 50 copies - for my director colleagues and friends serving on corporate boards."
– **Milton Carroll, Board Chair, HealthCare Service Corporation**

"Filled with practical tips and advice. Whether you are a new board member or an experienced director joining a new board, this book inspires you to shine brightly in the boardroom - from onboarding to taking on a board leadership role."
- **Deborah Rosati, Founder & CEO, Women Get on Board Corporate Director of TAAL (CSE: TAAL) and Khiron Life Sciences (TSVX: KHRN)**

"This captivating and insightful guide provides valuable insights as to how new and seasoned board members can navigate many complex issues facing the board. Practical yet thought provoking, this book belongs in every director's library."
– **Michael Millegan, Corporate Director of Coresite (NYSE:CORE), Portland General Electric (NYSE:POR), Axis Capital (NYSE:AXS)**

"Rich with straight-to-the-point practical ideas, typical of Beverly's candid style. It is a must-read not only for new directors; it serves as a good refresher for experienced directors, including those already in or taking up Committee or Board Chair roles."
– **Datuk Zaiton Mohd Hassan, Senior Independent Director, Sime Darby Plantation Bhd. Malaysia**

"I first invited Beverly to Colombia in 2011 after reading her very successful book, *Great Companies Deserve Great Boards*. Now she offers her readers *Becoming a Boardroom Star*, full of her personal experiences working with boards around the world for more than two decades. This book outlines the good practices that effective directors must master - and the bad habits they need to avoid. And she does it in a style that's easy to read and full of terrific anecdotes and great examples. This new book is a must for anyone involved in the corporate governance world."

 – **Ricardo Mejia, CEO of SALADEJUNTAS, Corporate Governance Professor and former director of 10 of the DINERO50 COMPANIES in Colombia.**

"An excellent roadmap for new directors who are learning to identify and navigate those fine lines separating management and oversight, going far beyond "noses in, fingers out" platitudes. Instead, it presents concrete suggestions for everything from new director onboarding to interfacing with management to assuming leadership roles within the board. In short, this book provides a comprehensive framework for directors – novice and veteran – who seek to maximize their value to their organizations."

 – **Teresa Matsui, CEO of Matsui Nurseries (one of the largest orchid companies in the world) and Director, Pacific Valley Bank**

"*Becoming a Boardroom Star* is a MUST read whether you're a new board member or have been serving on a board for some time. Based on her incomparable experience enhancing the effectiveness of boards around the globe (she's seen it all), Bev guides her readers to a deeper understanding of boards - what it takes to become a stand-out director, how to carry optimal director behaviors into committee and board leadership roles and more.

 – **Susan Colantuono, Founder, Leading Women**

BECOMING A BOARDROOM STAR

Beverly A. Behan
Board Advisor, LLC – New York

Copyright @ 2021 by Board Advisor, LLC

All rights reserved. No part of this publication may be reproduced, distributed, or transmitted in any form or by any means, including photocopying, recording, or other electronic or mechanical methods, without the prior written permission of the publisher, except in the case of brief quotations embodied in critical reviews and certain other noncommercial uses permitted by copyright law.

ISBN 978-1-7362161-8-7 eBook

ISBN 987-1-7362161-9-4 Audiobook

ISBN 978-1-7372295-4-4 Paperback

Board Advisor, LLC

New York, New York

www.boardadvisor.net

To contact the author with any questions or inquiries about working with you or your Board, speaking engagements, bulk orders of the book and/or for any other inquiries relating to this book or the subject matter herein, please Email: Beverly.behan@boardadvisor.net

Editor: Mary A. Metcalfe, M.S.

At A Glance....

Becoming a Boardroom Star is designed to offer practical advice and insights to directors who want to shine in the boardroom – earning the genuine esteem of their peers, the respect of senior management and, most importantly, adding real value for the organization they oversee. Not only is it brimming with ideas to help you raise your boardroom game and avoid common pitfalls, it's fun to read – a refreshing take on the sometimes stodgy world of governance.

Over the past 25 years, Beverly Behan has worked with nearly 200 Boards of Directors across the United States and around the world - from recent IPOs to the Fortune 500. Much of her work involved board and director evaluations, where board members spoke to her in confidence about the capabilities and contributions of their peers. She's interviewed more than a thousand directors about these issues. Becoming a Boardroom Star was developed from those discussions.

From New Directors to the Chair of the Board, this book offers genuinely worthwhile insights for directors at any stage of their boardroom career –be that in the Fortune 500, a private company or a local charity. It can help any board member to achieve a truly noble objective, that of becoming a boardroom star.

The book is divided into four Parts:

Part I: Becoming a Boardroom Star

This section discusses the increased expectations directors have of their fellow board members. Half the boards in America currently believe they have at least one "dog" – a director that should really be replaced. True boardroom stars aren't just strong individual contributors, they're great team players; a brilliant director who fails to understand that governance is a team sport will never truly shine in the boardroom. This section also discusses the five different board archetypes to help you determine the mode in which your board is currently operating – something that has important implications for the way you can be most impactful and effective as a member of that board.

Part II: Welcome to the Boardroom

This section discusses ways to enhance your director orientation – and pitfalls to avoid, including a chapter focused entirely on site visits. It also tackles one of the toughest transitions for any first-time director: making the shift from governance to management. Finally, it introduces the New Director 360, a new concept created for a Fortune 100 board in 2019 to make the most of its new director talent.

Part III: Hallmarks of a Boardroom Star

The opening chapter underscores the role model aspect of directorship and highlights key capabilities that distinguish true boardroom stars. Ten of the most common boardroom pitfalls are then discussed. Profiles in Boardroom Courage offers four case studies, ranging from a new director to committee chairs to a Lead Director, who all "did the right thing" and stepped up to a tough issue. Great directors at every stage of their board career can demonstrate the courage that distinguishes a true boardroom star.

Part IV: Board Leadership

Chairing a board committee - or the board itself - is an opportunity for a boardroom star to become a boardroom champion, someone in a board leadership role with a genuine commitment to excellence. An entire chapter offers practical advice on assuming a committee chair role; another focuses on the key facets of the Board Chair/Lead Director position. Director performance management – the area where most directors currently give board leadership their lowest scores – is discussed in-depth, including four director performance management tools every board leader should know about.

PART I
Becoming a Boardroom Star

Chapter One

STARS AND DOGS

OVER THE PAST 25 years, I've had the privilege of working with nearly 200 Boards of Directors across the United States and around the world. Much of this work involved board and director evaluations, where board members spoke to me in confidence about the capabilities and contributions of their peers. I've had conversations with more than a thousand directors about these issues - and this book was developed from those discussions.

It's designed to offer insights about what makes a great director shine in the boardroom – earning the genuine esteem of their peers, the respect of senior management and, most importantly, adding real value for the company's shareholders and other key stakeholders. We'll focus primarily on what distinguishes those directors considered truly outstanding from the others. But I'll also identify some of the pitfalls that new directors in particular should be careful to avoid.

It's interesting to note that for the past two years, a study of 700 US public company board members conducted by PriceWaterhouse Coopers found that 49% of respondents believe at least one of their fellow directors should be replaced; 21% believe that two or more need to go.[1,2] While almost every board has at least one star, the PwC findings suggest that in the view of directors themselves, at least half the boards in America currently have at least one "dog" as well.

During a recent podcast interview, I was asked if the PwC studies suggest director performance is getting worse. After all, when PwC researchers asked the same question in 2012, only 31% of respondents expressed the view that one of their fellow board members should be replaced.[3] I don't attribute the PwC results to a decline in director performance; rather, to the changing expectations of directors, themselves. Board members today are working harder than ever and facing unprecedented challenges. Because of this, I think they're more apt to critique a colleague who isn't carrying their weight.

I've seen tremendous improvement in most boards over the past two decades: The "country club" atmosphere that characterized most boardrooms in the twentieth century has long been a thing of the past. It's no longer acceptable to simply show up at board meetings and occasionally pipe up with, "Yes, I agree" to get your name in the minutes. Directors today want to make meaningful contributions – to leverage their experience, insights, and knowledge to benefit the organization they govern and guide it to success. And they expect the same from their peers.

Becoming a boardroom star begins with that mindset – a genuine desire to make a difference and a commitment to excellence. You already have that. How do I know? Because that's what made you decide to read this book.

As you read on, I hope the insights I can offer from two and half decades of working with hundreds of outstanding directors – and some "dogs" as well, if I'm totally honest – can help you to achieve your boardroom goals. I continue to believe what I wrote back in 2011: *Great Companies Deserve Great Boards* – and you can't build a great board without great directors.[4]

Chapter Two

GOVERNANCE IS A TEAM SPORT

AN EFFECTIVE BOARD functions as a high-performing governance team. Becoming a boardroom star requires a director to become an effective team player – whether they're new to the boardroom or serving as the Board Chair, Lead Director, or the chair of a board committee.

This may seem a bit counterintuitive to the traditional notion of stardom, which often refers to someone who shines in the limelight and exceeds their peers in accomplishment. But directors who seek to outshine their boardroom colleagues, "hog the airtime" in board meetings, revel in showing the rest of the board "how smart they are" and become almost giddy in playing "gotcha" with management – are seldom those described as boardroom stars. In fact, they're most often on the list of directors "who should probably be replaced."

A true boardroom star is typically described as a director who:

i. makes valuable contributions to board dialogue by asking critical questions and offering important insights and perspectives on the issues the board is dealing with; *and*

ii. plays a key role in supporting and advancing the effectiveness of the board as a team.

Once a director assumes a board leadership role – be that chairing a board committee or the board itself – their role in supporting the team becomes further amplified. Any director who harbors board leadership ambitions would do well to demonstrate these capabilities.

Below are some actual quotes about three boardroom stars who earned their fellow directors' esteem because they shone brightly as outstanding team players:

- "We recruited David, a recently retired Big Four partner, with the view that he would chair our Audit Committee when Ray, our current committee chair, retires. David is incredibly experienced and has a wealth of knowledge that frankly surpasses Ray's. But I really commend David for the way he's supported Ray over the past two years. David never tries to grandstand or show that he's smarter than Ray or more current on audit issues. He respects the fact that Ray continues to work hard as Audit Chair and spends a lot of time mentoring our young finance team. If David has a different perspective than Ray's, he's gracious when he introduces it. David is a class act. For me, the real issue now is this: David has shown such tremendous leadership that he's my top pick to become our next Board Chair. That leaves us having to find someone else to chair the Audit Committee because Ray's going to retire next year."

- "Miranda came on the board four years ago, shortly after she retired as a corporate executive and became president of a college in the Midwest. She knew a lot about our core business; she was in that field during her executive career. Last year, we decided to make a very large acquisition in an entirely new business which would become our growth platform. The entire board agreed that this was the right move for the company, albeit an ambitious one. But most of us had no background in the new business, ourselves. We knew that we needed to recruit some directors with experience in this new industry; in the meantime, we were doing our best to get up to speed. We asked management to put together some briefings to accelerate our learning. But they were swamped trying to integrate the companies. Miranda started doing some research about the new industry, herself; then she brought in some of her grad students to help. Within a few weeks, they created a briefing package for Miranda that she shared with the entire board and management. It contained a wealth of information on this new line of business – beautifully organized so that we could all quickly understand the key issues. This was absolutely tremendous!" *Note: Miranda has just been named successor to the current Board Chair – a unanimous board decision.*

- "Kirby was the Chief Technology Officer of [a Fortune 500 company] and has tremendous contacts in Silicon Valley. He's someone with a finger on the pulse of technology developments. Our IT team is not exactly what I'd call 'leading edge'. I could tell that Kirby was horrified when he saw how antiquated our systems were and what a challenge it would be for us to get up to speed, despite the recent hiring of an impressive new Chief Information Officer.

After Kirby had been on the board almost a year, Kirby did something that blew us all away: He took the new CIO and three of his top IT people to San Jose – and took them out to dinner with some of the biggest players in the Silicon Valley. Our team was meeting people way "out of their league" in the tech space; but Kirby had the contacts to give them that opportunity. It allowed our new CIO to forge relationships with these people – and he's been tapping into them ever since."

The team aspect of a board sometimes gets lost in the rush to address critical agenda items and get through the board meeting. As one director of an NYSE-listed retailer once told me: "Sometimes our board meetings feel like a 'hit and run' accident. You rush to the meetings from the airport, sit down and get into the issues, have some good debates and make important decisions – then rush back to the airport." I'm no fan of the 1980s country club style of governance that largely revolved around golf games and social events. But any team functions at its best when its players have built some camaraderie and rapport. Among other things, it fosters greater candor and openness; a director is far more likely to express an unpopular but heartfelt view to a group of people they've gotten to know, like, and trust. It can make a big difference in terms of the board's effectiveness, overall.

While you may not have the contacts to offer your IT team a dinner meeting with Silicon Valley luminaries or a cadre of grad students who can pump out a stellar industry analysis in a matter of weeks, you can nonetheless make an effort to get to know your fellow directors. It may require little more than making an effort to sit beside different board colleagues at every meeting, sharing an Uber ride with a director you barely know, or asking to have breakfast or lunch if you find yourself in another director's hometown.

Needless to say, these opportunities were restricted during the COVID-19 pandemic. But that didn't stop one creative board member, an economist, who invited his peers to a Zoom call to help him prepare for a webcast panel he'd agreed to serve on. The topic was, "The long-term impact of COVID-19 on the global economy". During the videoconference, fellow directors sipped wine and cocktails– and offered their thoughts on this issue, resulting in a wide-ranging and enjoyable discussion for all. At the end of the session, the Chair thanked the organizer profusely and told him, "It was wonderful to have a discussion with all these incredible people who serve on our board about a topic that doesn't directly relate to company business!"

Let's be clear: A director who has strong team skills but otherwise contributes little of value to board discussions will never be seen as a boardroom star. But neither will an insightful, brilliant director who is nonetheless a poor team player. Governance, after all, is a team sport.

Chapter Three

FIVE BOARD ARCHETYPES

TO BECOME A boardroom star, it can be important to first understand the type of board you're serving on. Board archetypes can provide a useful framework for analyzing the boardroom landscape, as illustrated in Figure 3.1:

Figure 3.1: Five Board Archetypes

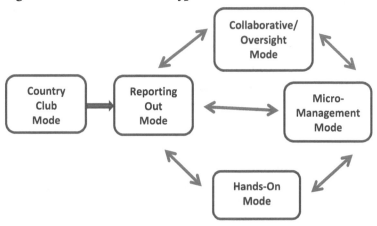

- ***Reporting-Out Mode:*** The majority of boards in the S&P1500 and other public companies around the globe currently operate in "Reporting Out" mode. The cadence of the board meetings typically involves the CEO and management "reporting out" to the board, seeking board approval for various initiatives, and entertaining directors' questions for further information and clarity. Management is essentially "telling" the board what's happening and what they're proposing - then responding to questions and challenges from directors, primarily defending their recommendations. The board is largely operating in an appropriate oversight role, making sure they have canvassed key risks, tested management's assumptions, and otherwise challenged a range of issues relative to the proposal before giving assent to management's recommendations.

- ***Collaborative/Oversight Mode:*** Dialogue in the board meetings is designed to engage directors in a robust two-way discussion with management, eliciting views from both management and the board around critical issues and assumptions underlying key decisions. Efforts are made by management to actively engage the board around particularly important issues where board expertise can be of genuine value to the management team – and where the board can make a real difference in providing guidance and/or confirming management's own points of view. The desired outcome is a final decision on a pivotal issue that board members and management thoroughly understand, largely (though not necessarily unanimously) support, and have provided their best thinking on. In this mode, the board plays a dual role as both: (i) a thought partner and collaborator, offering insights and sometimes even business contacts to management; and (ii) an effective overseer, challenging management where appropriate, and holding them accountable for achieving business goals and objectives.

- *Micro-Management Mode:* Board members delve into management-level details and weigh in on issues that would typically fall within the purview of management. This may characterize a board navigating a crisis – an "all hands on deck" scenario involving a corporate emergency such as the sudden departure of the CEO, a hostile takeover bid, or a major product failure resulting in a public relations nightmare. It was not at all uncommon to see boards adopt this operating mode during the COVID-19 pandemic in their efforts to help management navigate the unforeseen challenges of this situation. Boards also operate in this way when the board loses confidence in management, either due to performance problems or by directors feeling misled by the management team. Where trust becomes impaired, directors start to play "gotcha" with management – "drilling down" because of a concern that the CEO is hiding something from the board, which they hope to surface through astute and detailed questions.

- *Hands-On Mode:* The board routinely makes management-level decisions for implementation by the CEO and senior management. This is typical in early-stage companies where directors often provide expertise not yet resident within the executive team. It can work extremely well in these scenarios. A prolonged period of CEO/board disharmony in any company can also result in a board adopting this pattern – a shift from "short-term" to "long-term" micro-management. While the operating modes are similar, the tenor of these two Hands-On relationships is markedly different: largely positive and collaborative in the "early stage" scenario, highly contentious in the other.

- ***Country Club Mode:*** This characterized most boards in the 1980s and 1990s. Board service was viewed largely as an honorific appointment and directors enjoyed the perks and status of directorship while contributing relatively little in terms of their oversight of the organization. Board members were typically selected by the CEO, often long-time friends and business associates whose support the CEO could count on. Marquee directors were a mainstay of the S&P1500 at that time – "big names" who often served on multiple boards; sometimes eight or more! This wasn't difficult to manage as little was expected of those holding director roles at the time; corporate board members were often compared to the hood ornament on a Mercedes-Benz: "Impressive to look at but functionally useless". Enron became a pivot point for most public companies whose board members began to see their role as "a real job" and one of significant importance – requiring considerable time, effort, and a background/expertise that would allow a director to effectively challenge management's assumptions and proposals, recognize significant risks, and "call the question" on corporate leadership when things seemed amiss. Now exceedingly rare in the S&P1500, some founder-led companies and many non-profits continue to operate in Country Club mode, even today.

These operating modes are somewhat fluid: some boards will fluctuate between two or more of them in a single meeting. For example, the board may routinely operate in Reporting Out mode but lacks confidence in one corporate executive, causing directors to "jump the fence" into Micro-Management whenever this individual makes a presentation.

Most boards, however, have a predominant archetype. It can be useful to determine what that is, because it plays an important role in terms of establishing the norms for board members. For example, a board that typically operates in Reporting Out mode will be highly critical of directors who delve into micro-management, "wasting the board's time" with picayune details, and being overly directive in their approach. But at a board functioning in Hands-On or even Micro-Management mode, this is standard operating procedure.

Over the past two decades, we have witnessed an evolution of most public company boards from Country Club to Reporting Out mode, in which directors became far more engaged and felt compelled to make more worthwhile contributions in overseeing the company they governed than their counterparts of the late twentieth century. As Figure 3.1 illustrates, the evolution from Country Club to Reporting Out mode tends to be one-way; boards seldom revert back. And indeed, most boards today in the S&P1500 and other public companies around the world operate in Reporting Out mode.

It's worth noting, however, that many boards are now keen to make a further shift – one that involves a transition from the timeworn pattern of management Reporting Out to the board followed by, "Okay, any questions?" to a more collaborative approach focused on more robust two-way discussions of critical issues. After all, what's the point of recruiting directors who are successful corporate leaders, financial wizards, or technology innovators and then treating them largely as an audience for management presentations, with only the ability to ask a few questions at the end? That doesn't exactly harness the talent you've assembled in your boardroom. Collaborative/Oversight represents the next stage in a boardroom evolution that began twenty years ago with the fall of Enron. In the past several years, I've seen a real appetite to make this shift not only in boards across the US but around the world.

There are a number of important prerequisites necessary to effectively shift a board from Reporting Out to Collaborative/Oversight mode; I've outlined these in Appendix A. They're not "overnight changes" but can readily be achieved in two years or less with a champion Board Chair who sees real value in evolving the board in this way. However, this is not a book about board-building.[5] It's a book for individual directors who want to optimize their effectiveness in serving on any board fortunate enough to have them at the board table.

Let me conclude by saying this, however: Any boardroom star that shines brightly on a board largely operating in Reporting Out mode, will flourish if and when the board evolves to Collaborative/Oversight mode. The latter provides even greater opportunities for boardroom stars to leverage their knowledge, expertise, and insights. In fact, the more stars any board has, the more quickly management and board leadership will want to capitalize on their talents and capabilities by shifting to a Collaborative/Oversight approach.

PART II
Welcome to the Boardroom

Chapter Four

DRINKING FROM A FIREHOSE

OVER THE PAST two decades, director orientation has followed a similar format at companies around the world: The new director typically spends one or two days at company headquarters at the start of their board tenure. During this time, they meet with the Chief Executive Officer and other members of the C-suite, typically one after the next. Each executive provides an overview of their area of responsibility and discusses the major issues they're currently grappling with.

These meetings are important. They give the new board member "the lay of the corporate landscape" in terms of strategic direction, business imperatives, and key risks facing the company they've just signed on to oversee. They also provide an opportunity for the new director to meet the senior management team prior to working with them in the boardroom. And they're a million times better than director orientation practices of the past. In the 1990s, many new directors were simply handed a binder of materials and told to show up at the next board meeting. But the current format has its downsides. For many new directors, it becomes somewhat of a "drinking from a firehose" experience that leaves them valiantly trying to digest a dizzying download of important information as they're whisked from office to office on executive row.

Many boards are now rethinking the design of their director orientation programs. Most have added a site visit, where the new director visits a company facility – and many are increasingly creative in developing "hands-on" experiences for new directors to learn about the business, such as having them spend a morning on the front lines with a company technician or working the desk at one of their resorts. Some boards have now incorporated a second phase into their orientation program, to supplement the initial "executives on parade" format of phase one. Others have been redesigning their orientation programs to span the new director's entire first year on the board.

A Silver Lining

The COVID-19 pandemic curtailed the traditional "drinking from a firehose" orientation format. As many corporate facilities were locked down, and senior executives were working from home, the orientation briefings for directors recruited during this timeframe largely consisted of videoconferences. These could be scheduled intermittently, over several days or even weeks, allowing the new board member to catch their breath between these meetings. And the briefings no longer needed to be scheduled back-to-back, allowing for more relaxed dialogue; if one conversation ran overtime, another executive wasn't inconvenienced by the delay.

Site visits became a challenge during COVID-19; both lockdowns and travel restrictions kept new board members away from manufacturing facilities, warehouses, and other field operations. However, many boards solved that problem with videos. While a video may not have the same impact as walking through the plant, the lab, the orchard, or the mine, it allowed more sites to be included. New directors didn't need to travel; they could watch these videos from the comfort of their home office. Many longer-serving directors asked to see them as well.

One silver lining of the COVID-19 lockdowns from a board perspective has been the newfound comfort that directors and executives developed with videoconferencing. Zoom and its cousins – MicroSoft Teams, BlueJeans, and others – can now be utilized in director orientation and other board processes, such as board evaluations, even after the lockdowns have ended. This opens up approaches that were never considered prior to 2020.

For example, a new director could now easily hold 45-minute Zoom calls with the chair of each board committee to learn more about the committee's current focus and key decisions; earlier, this would have necessitated the scheduling of face-to-face meetings and probably some travel, given that many board members live in different parts of the country and sometimes even different parts of the world. Expanding a new director's orientation program, at least to some extent, has never been easier.

Designing Your Own Orientation Program

Boardroom stars never criticize or refuse to participate in the company's director orientation program; they merely look for ways to expand their orientation to make it even more worthwhile. After all, the faster any new director learns about the company and its business, the sooner they can start to make meaningful contributions in the boardroom.

Here are some of the questions you might want to consider in determining a few additional orientation topics that could be useful to explore:

- Is there an issue that was discussed almost "in passing" during your initial meetings with C-suite executives that you'd like to delve into more deeply?

- Is there a topic that emerged during your first one or two board meetings that you'd like to learn more about – so that you don't take up a lot of board meeting time asking questions?

- Would you find it helpful to spend some time with management in the area of your core expertise, be it technology, finance, or logistics? Or in an area that you know very little about?

Every time you ask for an additional briefing in your director orientation, be mindful of the fact that it will require time and effort by someone in management to prepare for and conduct the session. For this reason, it's important to be selective. Focus on topics that would genuinely be of value for you to learn more about as a board member such as (i) issues that will have a real bearing on the company's success and will likely be a focal point of board discussions going forward; or (ii) issues that pose significant risks to the company which, as a director, you'd do well to more fully understand.

And be careful not to overdo it. No new director wants to come across as:

- A prima donna – imposing on management's time for endless meetings to review different facets of the business; or

- An economic tourist – flying First Class to visit corporate sites across the country or around the world on the company's nickel, all in the name of "director education".

A potential star can become a dog pretty quickly in those circumstances.

Be Inclusive

Your "new director" status gives you the privilege of being able to ask for some additional briefings for orientation purposes, often on topics that incumbent directors would also value learning more about. Let's say you've asked for a 45-minute briefing on the company's investment in a new water purification system that seems to be a cornerstone of the corporate growth strategy. The entire board was briefed on the project when they were asked to approve the investment last year. You could suggest that your orientation briefing be opened up to any other directors who might want to join in; after all, if management is going to create a session for you, there should be no additional work required on their part if other board members wish to participate as well.

Make it clear, however, that extending the invitation to other directors is management's decision. Don't argue if they ask to limit the briefing to you, alone; there might be a reason for that. For example, the project might have been going sideways and the CEO is still exploring the reasons for this and not yet ready to engage in a discussion with the full board about the problem. In most cases, however, management will think it's a great idea – and so will many of your board colleagues.

One director who took this approach was startled when nearly half the board showed up at his briefing on an international project. In fact, they were grateful not only that he'd set up this session – but that he suggested it be extended to other directors who might want to join. "This was just great, Rick!" one of the director's new board colleagues told him at the end of the briefing, "What are you going to ask for an orientation session on next? Can we offer some ideas?"

Get a Good Overview on Your Area of Expertise

Boards today have become far more sophisticated about board composition. In selecting you as a new director, the board undoubtedly felt that your background would be particularly valuable at the board table. Whether your expertise is in information technology, brand marketing, or auditing, when an item that's squarely within your wheelhouse emerges on the board agenda, they'll be counting on you to weigh in. If you've got a legal background, for example, they'll certainly expect to hear your perspectives in discussions on a shareholder lawsuit. If you're a marketing guru, they'll want you to offer some important insights when the board is asked to approve an investment in a new platform that dramatically changes the customer online experience. Many directors extoll their boardroom stars who contribute in this way: "Sometimes I think the board is a bit too reliant on Pam when it comes to capital structure issues, because we always know "Pam's got this". But it's sure nice to have that kind of confidence in a board member. We're very fortunate that way."

Because of these expectations, it can be particularly important to learn more about the company's approach and initiatives in your area of expertise during your orientation. Doing so can provide you with some context and history that can be critical in making effective contributions when these issues arise in board meetings.

Boards that have adopted a two-phase director orientation program often focus phase two around the new director's area of expertise: a new board member with a finance background might spend half a day with the internal and external auditors. A new director with a technology background might visit with the team responsible for an artificial intelligence program.

One Fortune 100 Lead Director commented on the importance of this component of director orientation relative to a new board recruit who he believed was destined to become a boardroom star: "Greg is one of the foremost thought leaders in the country, if not the world, on this topic. If Greg were to have coffee with our team working on this project, he'd learn more in half an hour than he'd hear about for months in the boardroom. Then Greg's up to speed when this issue arises in the board meetings; he's not asking questions in there trying to understand the context and history of the project. I know the CEO plans to tap into Greg's insights in this area off-line of the meetings; he's excited about that, in fact. And Greg will be a much more valuable resource for the CEO, the more he knows at the outset about our work in this area. Besides, who on the management team working on this project wouldn't want to have coffee with Greg?! He's a rock star in this field!"

The truth is, most senior managers are delighted to have coffee, meetings, or any other interface with board members. It also "humanizes" the board, which employees often perceive as a lofty, intimidating, and rather shadowy group. Unpopular policies within many companies are frequently blamed on "the board". It can be helpful for them to meet directors from time to time and learn that they're not only smart and impressive, in most cases they're really nice people who genuinely want the company to be successful.

Now, one very important note of caution about these types of meetings – which applies to all interactions between directors and senior management: A director should try to scrupulously avoid giving opinions, advice and/or (egads!) direction to management in these briefings.

This can be a bit nuanced, at times. One boardroom star – the CFO of a Fortune 500 company – explained how easily she might have fallen into this trap almost inadvertently when she met with the internal audit team during her director orientation:

> The meeting was great – really informative and helpful for me as a new director. The conversation eventually drifted into an area where there's been a lot of debate. The head of internal audit asked me, "How did you decide to handle this particular issue at your company?" We had taken a different approach. And I was all set to tell him what we'd chosen to do and why – and to extoll the merits of our decision, which I'd given a lot of thought to personally.
>
> Fortunately, I stopped myself. I realized that if I responded in that way, he'd go running to the CFO as soon as the meeting was over and tell him that I saw things quite differently on this issue, potentially reopening a tough debate and casting doubt on the CFO's decision on this matter. I knew how I'd feel, as CFO, if someone on the board at my company put me in that position. It wouldn't start us off on a good footing. And I fully appreciated that there are many factors to consider relative to handling this particular issue; that's what made it contentious. There was nothing troubling about the decision they'd made; it was largely a matter of opinion. My opinion just happened to differ when I had to consider the question at my own company.

So, instead, I responded this way: "We took a somewhat different approach. But there are many considerations to take into account in deciding how best to handle this question. What I'd like to understand are the factors that led to the decision you and your team ended up making – and which your external auditors obviously support."

Crisis averted.

Chapter Five

SITE VISITS

SITE VISITS ARE important, particularly for new directors who have not previously worked in the industry of the company they're about to govern. While videos can provide terrific exposure to a range of company facilities, many new directors will say, "The business really came to life for me when I walked through …" our new factory in Dayton, our farming operations in Maryland, our mine in Colorado, our laboratories outside of Boston. Employees often take pride in the fact that a board member has considered their operations to be worthy of a visit.

One complaint I frequently hear from CEOs goes something like this: "Most of our board members have never even taken the time to walk through one of our plants on their own – not even the new plant in Dayton. You'd think a director might say, "Hey, I'd like to go and see this new plant that the board approved all that money to create!" The only way we can get the board out to a plant is to plan a board meeting there. Now, that can be a good idea, but it's very expensive. We have to fly our whole executive team to the plant as well as the board and pay for accommodations, etc. So, we only hold board meetings at corporate sites once a year; at that rate, it would take fifteen years to see every one of our major facilities! I'd just like my directors to take some initiative in terms of getting out to see the different aspects of our business. After all, they're overseeing the business; that's their job."

Most requests from a director to visit a company site will earn kudos from the management team and fellow board members. But as with additional orientation briefings, it's important to be judicious about the number of site visits requested and to consider the optics of your selections. For example, making time to visit the new plant in Dayton will undoubtedly be viewed as an excellent initiative – and is likely to be a great learning experience for the director who makes the trip. A request to explore the company's small field office in Honolulu, on the other hand, will be seen as a thinly disguised excuse for a glamorous trip at the company's expense, with little educational value.

Boardroom stars often use their own personal or business travel to facilitate a visit to a company site or even to attend an industry conference. This is a terrific practice that a board member can adopt at any stage in their tenure; it's certainly not limited to orientation.

Management is usually thrilled when directors take these initiatives and typically respond with comments like: "Scott made the time to visit our plant in Salt Lake City by working it into his trip there a few months back; he did the same thing with our warehouse in Atlanta when he was visiting his daughter. To me, these efforts demonstrate that Scott really cares about the company. When the board's looking at an investment or some other issue impacting one of the sites Scott's visited, he'll often chime in and say, 'You know, I've been there, and I can see what they're concerned about' or some other comment that reflects his own observations from his visit. I wish more directors would take this kind of initiative."

Directors who work site visits into their travel schedule also comment that it gives them an 'unvarnished' look at the facilities: "One thing I like about making arrangements to stop by a company site when I'm travelling is that I see the site exactly how it is. When we plan a board meeting at a company facility, you always know that efforts have been made to 'pretty up' the site for the board – you can almost smell the fresh coats of paint."

But what if you don't boast a travel schedule that readily lends itself to company site visits? Simply ask if you can visit the new plant in Dayton – or whatever your own equivalent might be. And here's my recommendation when you do so: Offer to pay your own travel expenses if management will arrange the visit. No, of course you shouldn't have to; this is company business after all. And management will probably be delighted that you offered to take time out of your busy schedule to visit a company facility. But particularly in circumstances where the organization has been weathering some financial challenges, it's a smart thing to do – and typically earns the director so much goodwill that it's worth every dime.

Don't be surprised if the company insists on covering your costs – they very often do; they might even provide the corporate jet to take you to and from the visit. But the point is this: You asked to go, and you offered to pay – which demonstrates your willingness and commitment to invest in learning about the company and its business.

Site Visits can Include Websites Too!

One boardroom star took another initiative to learn more about the company's major competitors without even leaving her home office.

Kelly spent a weekend hunkered down with her laptop, Internet shopping on competitors' sites.

> This experience brought the business to life for me; it gave me sort of a visual of things I'd been hearing about. We have a niche customer segment and that became very evident the more time I spent on this research. I could clearly see how we were trying to differentiate ourselves on-line. For many of our competitors, this business – which is our core business – appeared to be a sideline to an extensive product list. I'd heard that multiple times during my orientation briefings but going on these websites really drove this point home to me.
>
> I bought products from our site and from our competitors. I wanted to see what the check-out process was like, how fast it took for the items to arrive, even how they were packaged. And of course, I could compare our products with those of our competition, although I'll admit I didn't order from all eight of the competitors whose websites I explored – only about half of them.

At the end of her research, Kelly wrote up her notes and sent them to the CEO and the head of marketing with an important caveat:

> I thought my observations might be helpful, so, why not pass them along, rather than just filing my notes away and putting all the stuff I ordered at the back of a closet? But I didn't want the CEO or the CMO to feel they had to do anything with this information – or even respond to me. I think management always worries when they get a note from a director that this is some new 'make work' project for them and that's the last thing I wanted to create.
>
> So, I wrote this at the top of the first page: "I spent the weekend combing through many of our competitors' websites as a

step in my own orientation as a new director. I am sharing my notes with you only because I hope they may be helpful and of interest; if you'd like me to send you any of the competitors' products that I ordered, I'd be happy to do so, although I suspect you do this sort of thing yourselves. Please do not feel any need to follow up with me or take any action whatsoever; these notes are purely for your information. I hope they are useful."

The CEO and CMO were "blown away" by Kelly's initiative to learn more about the competitive landscape. And they particularly appreciated her cover note; it underscored her understanding of the governance/management line and her respect for management's time and priorities. The CEO asked Kelly if she'd share a 10-minute overview of her experience and observations with the other directors at an upcoming board meeting. Her process and insights were so well-received that "competitor website research" became a formal component of the company's director orientation program thereafter.

"He Left as a Board Member – and Returned as a Building Inspector"

One critical issue to bear in mind about site visits is that their fundamental purpose is director education: they give board members an opportunity to better understand the business by setting foot in the company facilities and seeing different facets of the company's operations. Although management and other board members generally applaud the efforts of directors to visit company sites, this can sour quickly if a board member loses sight of this objective.

A classic instance of a site visit gone awry involved Max, a former engineer who'd run a major division of a global firm in his executive career. Max had been on the board for several years but had never visited any of the company's facilities; in fairness, management had been lax about organizing trips for directors and never held board meetings anywhere other than the company's headquarters. Having recently attended a governance conference where other directors endorsed the merits of site visits, Max took the initiative to visit the company's facility in the Midwest.

A week after his trip, Max circulated a laundry list of twenty-three recommendations for improvements at the plant to the CEO and other members of the board. These ranged from increasing the number of stalls for Visitor Parking to better washroom signage. Most directors simply chuckled when reviewing Max's notes. But Max was on a mission; he began haranguing the CEO for commitments on his recommended changes. Max had enjoyed himself so much on his first site visit, in fact, that he started planning another one. It was then that the CEO pleaded with the Lead Director to intervene.

"Max left as a board member – and returned as a building inspector," the Lead Director joked, when recalling the incident, "I had to sit down with Max and explain that the purpose of a site visit is for the director's enlightenment, to help them better understand and get a feel for the business. By returning from Cleveland with this long list of recommendations – albeit with a genuine desire to create improvements – Max was not only micro-managing, he was annoying and distracting the management team. We didn't send him to Cleveland as a consultant; we sent him to see the plant, so that he had a visual of the facility that the board just allocated $120 million to expand."

While Max's approach clearly missed the mark, an even more awkward situation can be created when a board member starts giving direction to employees during the site visit itself. This doesn't mean that a director should ignore evident safety concerns or other significant issues they might come across on a site visit. They should, of course, point those out right away – or raise them with the CEO or Chair/Lead Director immediately upon their return. But these issues are relatively rare in my experience.

Another important consideration on site visits is this: Whenever directors interact with employees and managers below the C-suite level, they can become the target of disgruntled employees with an axe to grind. Whether it's changes to the bonus program, budget cuts, or the firing of a "long time and loyal employee", the more often a director ventures into the field, the more likely they are to face these types of complaints. It can be useful to ask the CEO or whoever is arranging your site visit if there are any contentious issues involving this facility that could emerge while you're there. That way, you'll be somewhat more prepared if you hear about them during your visit. (As a director, it can also be eye-opening to simply hear about some issues at company sites that seem to be causing a bit of a stir).

If an employee complaint *does* arise while you're at the facility, the best strategy is often simply to listen and ask questions for clarification. It's seldom a good idea to take a position – even if you have some additional facts on the matter from a pre-visit briefing; this is management's headache, and it's unwise to start micro-managing the matter by getting personally involved. "I'll mention this to the CEO; I'm glad you raised it," is nearly always the best type of response.

And indeed, you probably should follow up with the CEO when you return, particularly if this was an issue that management anticipated would be "hot button" during your visit. Let them know what happened – and what was said when the matter was mentioned to you, without creating some sort of "witch hunt" for the employee who stepped forward; they probably did so with the very best of motives. If you were blasted about changes to the bonus program, you could let the Chair of the Compensation Committee know about that, as well; there's nothing wrong with that. Besides, if you're a new director, it may be useful to find out what went on with those changes to the bonus program; it was obviously a difficult and contentious board decision. But just as you want to avoid returning from any site visit as a building inspector, so too should you resist the temptation to return as an employee ombudsperson.

Now, if an employee raises a concern involving significant misconduct – fraud, sexual harassment, or the like – that's a very different issue than someone grousing about their bonus or the fact that their budget was cut, or their friend was laid off. Serious allegations cannot be ignored. Take the matter up with the leader of the independent directors – be that the Non-Executive Chair or Lead Director. Depending on the circumstances, you may need to call in the General Counsel or even outside legal counsel to determine if an investigation is warranted and/or what the best approach may be.

Repeated complaints about similar types of issues may also warrant some scrutiny. For example, one disgruntled employee bemoaning the "insensitive treatment" of a former colleague is one thing; but repeated allegations of this nature may suggest a larger problem, and a troubling corporate culture issue. Again, the leader of the independent directors should probably be your first call if you encounter this type of situation. These issues typically require some investigation before you can determine whether there really *is* a significant concern, what it involves, and how best to address it.

Chapter Six

NOSE IN, FINGERS OUT

ONE OF THE biggest challenges for any first-time director is understanding the line between governance and management. It's natural for a current or former executive to sit down in a board meeting and start asking the same sorts of questions they'd raise in a C-suite discussion at their own company. But in doing so, they're typically operating in management mode. Governance is all about overseeing management in running the company – not running the company yourself. This is the steepest "learning curve" for many new directors when they move from the executive suite to the boardroom.

The management/governance line is not an easy one to master. There are many definitions, most highlighting the difference between strategic issues (governance) and tactical or operational issues (management). But in reality, the line can become rather blurry. Jan Masaoka jokingly defines micro-management in the non-profit governance blog *Blue Avocado* as "whatever the board is doing that the executive director (or CEO) doesn't like"[6] while other authors point out that "For many directors, micro-management is often thought of as inconsequential; a little bit of fine-tuning here and an extended discussion there. It has all the hallmarks of a thorough and prudent board member securing down the facts and details."[7]

Micro-management is often a more troubling problem at non-profit organizations than in the corporate world. Here's a terrific example from an author who advises non-profit boards:

> Micro-managing board members show up to their first board meeting and before they have done anything of substance for the organization, they want to revamp the reports, review the non-profit's journal, question every expense, and critique the Chief Executive's management style.[8]

This is one of the reasons that executives who seek to gain some initial governance experience by serving on non-profit boards need to be somewhat cautious about translating that experience directly to the corporate boardroom. Non-profit boards are a different animal, often comprised of large donors and volunteers, who by their very nature – and usually with the best of intentions – tend to "get into the weeds". But that's not to say that you won't encounter micro-managing boards in the corporate world; you most certainly will. As noted in the earlier discussion on the Five Board Archetypes, corporate boards tend to micro-manage in the following scenarios:

- **A Corporate Crisis:** Whether this involves a dramatic loss of revenue, a significant product failure, a spate of negative headlines, or the sudden loss of the CEO, most board members quite rightly "roll up their sleeves" in an emergency situation and become intensely involved, doing all they can to try to help management address the situation and "right the corporate ship".

- **Loss of Trust/Confidence in Management:** In these situations, management has either stunned the board with a negative "surprise", repeatedly failed to keep their promises, or has played "fast and loose" with the board, by hiding some important information that ultimately came back to haunt them. A good example of the latter was a CEO who desperately wanted board approval of a major acquisition; he "buried" one of the biggest risks of the deal in a single sentence on page 44 of the board briefing book, in a way that could be easily overlooked. When the risk "came home to roost", he smugly pointed directors to page 44. I'm sure you can imagine the boardroom grilling he got on every proposal thereafter.

- **A Start-Up/Early-Stage Company:** This is the classic Hands-On archetype described in Chapter Three – where the founder uses the board as a quasi-executive team, drawing on the expertise of board members for decisions in areas that would ordinarily fall to management. This approach works very successfully at early-stage companies – but would be considered anathema at a more mature organization. Down the road, when the founder departs, their successor will almost inevitably express frustration about the board's blatant micro-management; but transitioning a Hands-On board to operate at a governance level is a board-building issue. There is, however, an important implication: If most of your board experience to date has involved early-stage companies, don't be surprised if you find the governance/management line a bit tough to navigate should you subsequently join the board of a more well-established S&P1500.

"Will It Be a Brown Squirrel or a Gray One?"

There's another scenario where many corporate boards end up "getting into the weeds" of micro-management: management takes them there. Some board books include "everything but the kitchen sink" – and some executives load up their board presentations with a host of minor details as well.

In one workshop I conducted for senior executives of a Fortune 500 company on improving their boardroom effectiveness, we used a simplistic example in an unrelated industry: The product launch of a new brand of peanut butter. Appropriate governance level issues for this scenario were quite properly identified as: the level of investment required, the size of the market, the strategic plan for market penetration, channels of distribution, management capability/infrastructure/resources required to execute the plan, likely competitive response, projected sales volumes, and return on investment.

Examples of micro-management included: the size of the jars, the product description and whether the company would feature a squirrel or a chipmunk in its advertising. Most directors can't resist this type of delicious detail if it's offered: "Oh, squirrels are the way to go! Will it be a brown squirrel or a gray one?" Just then, one of the executives exclaimed: "OMG! I just realized what went wrong at my last board presentation. I ended up spending half an hour talking to the board about "gray squirrels" – with hardly any time spent on the critical issues. I walked out of that meeting completely frustrated. But I'm the one that teed up the 'squirrel conversation'."

In nearly 200 board evaluations that I've conducted over the past 25 years, two-thirds identified board pre-reading materials as an area for improvement. Be it the Midwestern REIT that provided "move in/move out" data on every one of their two hundred apartment buildings; the North American restaurant chain that littered their board books with the financials of each of their forty bistros; or the Asian conglomerate that incorporated multiple red-lines of modified corporate policies as a routine feature of their pre-reading packages – all these companies took their boards "into the weeds" and then expressed dismay that the board "is always asking us about stupid little details that don't even matter!"

If your board materials are filled with "stupid little details that don't even matter" my best advice is this: Don't take the bait. Yes, the board books should be improved; any board that's wading through minutiae is rarely operating at the top of its game. But that's a board-building issue. In the meantime, you need to ignore these kinds of juicy details, resist the temptation to ask about "squirrels", focus on the strategic issues, and keep your boardroom questions at an oversight level.

Board Buddies

Adapting to an oversight role is one of the toughest transitions any executive has to make when they accept their first outside board seat. So, how can a new director get a solid grasp of the governance/management line? Lectures and hand-outs seldom work. Most definitions, including the beloved "nose in, fingers out" and "strategic vs tactical" are hardly a bright line test, especially when board debates start swirling around some inordinately complex issues. But "board buddies" do – if the newbie and the incumbent routinely connect before every board meeting during the new director's first year.

Board buddies was a concept that entered the governance lexicon ten years ago. It's a practice whereby a new director is assigned to a longer-serving member of the board as their "buddy". The original concept was that the buddy could give the new director some context and background relative to items on the board agenda – even some of the board/management politics surrounding the more contentious issues. This alone, is a very good reason for adopting a board buddy program: it can alert a new director to potential boardroom minefields and avoid rehashing issues that the board has already covered in-depth prior to the new director's arrival.

Several years ago, however, I began noticing board buddy programs taking on another dimension when the new director was a first-timer on a corporate board: not only would the buddy provide some history relative to the board agenda items, but they would also serve as a sounding board for "test questions" from the new director. If the question was squarely aimed at a management level issue, the buddy could offer suggestions on how it might be reframed to get to the crux of the issue the new director wants to address, yet focus at an oversight level. In my experience, after three or four of these sessions, most new directors will typically have mastered the governance/management line.

This is the best and most practical approach I've ever seen. If you're a first-time director and your board doesn't have a board buddy program, consider asking the Chair of the Nominating and Governance Committee for this kind of support from one of your new colleagues. I suspect you'll find it helpful on many levels, so long as you and your buddy have the discipline to regularly schedule these conversations prior to the meetings. A simple "Call me if you need any help" will seldom achieve very much.

If you're a longer-serving director still struggling with the governance/management line, consider reaching out to a board colleague for similar support. You can either adopt the pattern of connecting prior to board meetings, described earlier, or, because you won't need any background or context on the agenda items, you and your buddy could decide to debrief after the meetings. When you do, ask for some feedback about the questions you raised: Did they seem to be at an oversight level? Would your buddy have asked the question(s) differently? Or would they have avoided some of the topics you got into altogether? And if so, why?

Don't be hesitant or embarrassed to ask for a little help around this issue. Mastering the governance/management line is one of the biggest challenges for many directors – and a bit of "real time" feedback is the most practical device to address it, so long as your buddy has a clear understanding of the line, themselves. Even today, you will encounter directors who've served on boards for ten years or more that still appear to be struggling with the governance/management line. They are seldom viewed as boardroom stars.

Chapter Seven

NEW DIRECTOR 360s

IN 2019, I was asked to undertake a director evaluation process by a Fortune 100 company that had recently recruited two very sophisticated new board members with extensive experience on other Fortune 500 boards. They had served for twelve and eighteen months, respectively. As both were considered potential boardroom stars, the Chair of the Nominating and Governance Committee wanted this exercise to be genuinely worthwhile for them – a vehicle designed to make the most of this terrific new director talent. So, we designed a process that went "above and beyond" a typical director evaluation. I now call it the New Director 360.

Three things distinguish a New Director 360 from a regular director evaluation process:

➢ New Director 360s are more comprehensive than a regular director evaluation, as illustrated by the sample feedback report included at Appendix B. This is because a New

Director 360 involves an expanded range of interviewees: all members of the board, several executives who regularly work with the board and its committees, and external advisors who have worked with the new director during their first 12–18 months - external auditors, and/or compensation consultants.

➢ Receiving constructive feedback from the rest of the board can be particularly meaningful for new directors, even those who already have significant board experience. It reinforces what peers and colleagues already see as their strengths and contributions to date, enabling them to both recognize and capitalize on these things. It can also nip any performance problems in the bud. Some directors do get off to a rocky start – and it's far easier to address these issues early on than have them fester. Constructive, actionable feedback – along the lines of Appendix B – is far more useful than generic comments such as, "You've been a great addition to our board!" or "Things haven't started off the way we'd hoped, but I'm sure they'll improve", which is typically all that a new director gets without a structured process.

➢ The New Director 360 is both evaluative *and* developmental in nature. Interviewees are specifically asked for suggestions that could contribute to the new director's continued development post-orientation. This can generate some very innovative ideas along the lines of those discussed in Chapters Four and Five: visits to specific company locations, attendance at an industry conference that may be particularly worthwhile, ways in which the new director can best leverage their own subject matter expertise and network to benefit the company and its management team.

For an aspiring boardroom star, the New Director 360 may be the perfect capstone of your orientation program, providing you with genuinely worthwhile feedback while underscoring to the board your own commitment to professional development. If you feel that a New Director 360 would be worthwhile, there's nothing stopping you from asking the Chair of the Nominating and Governance Committee about the idea. It's likely to be more valuable to you personally, than most director education seminars – and no one else on the board even needs to see your feedback.

Leading by Example

A few weeks ago, I received a call from a boardroom star I've had the pleasure of working with in the past. Julie recently joined another S&P1500 board. She'd only attended two meetings so far, but it was evident that the Chair of her new board was struggling. She wanted to help but recognized the importance of taking the right approach. Here's how Julie described the problem:

> The Chair opens the board meetings by giving a speech – which goes on for more than half an hour. This is not a Chair setting up the board meeting with an overview of the agenda items, the theme of the meeting or things that have happened in the company since the board last met. This is like the Gettysburg Address. There's only five minutes allocated on the board agenda for the Chair's Opening Remarks, so the meeting is really running behind from the very start.
>
> Then, once we get underway, people drift into all kinds of extraneous topics – and the Chair just lets it roll. It took us ninety minutes to get to a decision on the first agenda item, which was not contentious. Even then, the CEO had to repeatedly ask, "Is the board now saying that we can move forward – or not? I just

need to be clear." And he was right; the board was not clear. The meeting was scheduled as a five-hour videoconference; we ended up running two hours overtime. We put off two decisions on items that I could tell management really needed an answer on. But we'd been at it for seven hours, and people had to leave!

The CEO is really fed up; apparently management makes jokes about the Chair and how he runs the board meetings. I really like the Chair personally. He's a nice man who is well-intentioned and absolutely loves the company. But these meetings are a disaster! Another director who's very frustrated serves on the Governance Committee. Last year, the Committee tried to introduce director evaluations, but the Chair stonewalled their efforts. I'm not sure what else to suggest or if I should even get involved; after all, I'm the "new kid on the block".

The Governance Committee had been on the right track with the idea of a director evaluation. Even a well-designed board evaluation, using comprehensive well-structured interviews, instead of a survey format, would have provided an effective platform to address these issues in a constructive way. But it was clear that the Chair wasn't open to these ideas; little would be gained for Julie to revisit them.

So, I made an entirely different suggestion: A New Director 360 – for Julie – once she'd completed her first year on the board. No, it wouldn't address the real problem. But it might demonstrate to the Chair – and to other board members– that a director evaluation can be genuinely helpful and nothing to fear. The Chair, the CEO and other directors would, of course, be interviewed for Julie's New Director 360, giving them first-hand experience with the process.

If Julie decides to move forward with this idea after she's served on the board a few more months, I suspect her new board colleagues will both appreciate her openness to feedback and admire her commitment to continuous improvement. If, when the exercise concludes, Julie shares some of her feedback and indicates how the process was useful to her, that might go a long way to convincing the Chair and other directors to reconsider the benefits of director evaluations. Even as a new board member, Julie can nonetheless lead by example – which is exactly what boardroom stars do.

PART III

Hallmarks of a Boardroom Star

Chapter Eight

BOARDROOMS ARE LIKE FISHBOWLS

THE BOARD OF Directors sets the ultimate tone at the top of any organization. If the organization has a set of corporate values that include "excellence", "teamwork", and "mutual respect", what are executives to think if they walk into a board meeting and see directors who are unprepared, disengaged, and snarky to their colleagues? It diminishes the board's credibility and that of the organization itself.

Boardroom stars strive to be role models. They conduct themselves in a way that earns the genuine respect of their peers and of the management team. They don't rely on laurels from earlier accomplishments, however impressive those might be; they earn respect from the way they behave and perform as a board member. The concept of board service as some kind of reward or honor for a lifetime of business achievement is a twentieth century artifact that went up in smoke twenty years ago, alongside a company known as Enron.

Most directors today work hard and have high expectations of their boardroom colleagues. The more venerable a director's reputation, the higher the board's hopes – and those of management – in terms of the contributions they can make in the boardroom.

Work Ethic

It's readily apparent to directors and management alike, which directors invest the time and effort that should be expected of anyone serving on a Board of Directors – and which do not. There are two requirements of board members when it comes to work ethic:

- First, you need to prepare for board and committee meetings so that you can weigh in during the meetings with pertinent questions, valuable insights, and worthwhile comments on the agenda items under discussion. If there's an item that requires a board decision, you should be prepared to make that decision. Or, if you feel you can't, you need to address that beforehand.

- Second, it's important to keep abreast of relevant developments in the economy, the company's industry, and the competitive landscape. This provides context that any director requires to effectively oversee a company; it also yields a better understanding of emerging risks and opportunities that can impact the organization. You also need to keep current on governance issues – "hot topics" for shareholders, best practices, and innovations in both board effectiveness and in the relevant area of each board committee on which you serve.

A director who takes time well in advance of the board meeting to carefully review the materials, reflect on the key items on the agenda, and develop a list of thoughtful questions and comments, typically comes across quite differently than someone who's tried to hastily digest the board book and jot down a few thoughts on the flight to the meeting. Don't kid yourself – it shows. A director who makes an effort to stay up to date on the industry will more readily understand the context of competitive moves, consumer trends and/or regulatory proposals when they emerge in board discussions. That shows, too.

Studies suggest that public company directors spend roughly 250 hours per year on board-related matters, which is roughly a month of time on an annual basis.[9] The time requirement for committee chairs is significantly more – and even greater for a Lead Director or Board Chair. Boards in the S&P500 typically meet between six and nine times a year and most have four standing committees,[10] which often meet about the same number of times as the board itself. There can also be ad hoc or special board committees, such as CEO Succession Planning, which can be extremely time-consuming. And if the company is facing a crisis, there will be board calls on a weekly and sometimes even daily basis, depending on the circumstances. Directors are expected to be available; this is a time when the company and its stakeholders need "all hands on deck".

In the non-profit world, a guideline seems to have developed that board members of charities, universities, and other not for profit entities should anticipate spending at least 5–10 hours a month on board-related business.[11] And again, this commitment will amplify if a director assumes a committee chairmanship or other board leadership role and/or if the organization faces some type of emergency, such as allegations of misconduct, a sudden loss of leadership, or a deluge of bad press.

Pick Your Spots

Most corporate board meetings run about 4–6 hours and there's generally a lot to cover.[12] The director who "hardly says anything" or who "only speaks to get their name in the minutes – once at every meeting, like clockwork" is clearly not making a worthwhile contribution. But the boardroom "air hog," who feels compelled to weigh in on every agenda item, isn't well-regarded either. Board meeting time is precious. And making the most of it often comes down to one piece of conventional wisdom: Pick your spots.

Preparation is the key. Determine which agenda items you most want to ask about or offer a viewpoint on, then develop and prioritize those questions and comments. If someone makes that point before you do, move on to the next item. Try to avoid being one of those board members whose comments seldom involve more than agreeing with a point that's already been made. When you speak up in a meeting, try to offer a fresh perspective or different question that hasn't yet been addressed.

Don't feel the need to weigh in on every item; this is a rookie mistake: "You can tell that this is Matt's first board. Someone needs to tell him that a board member doesn't have to express a view on every single item on the agenda. It's almost painful to watch!" That said, it's important to formulate a position on every major item, whether you choose to express it in the meeting or not. On significant issues, it's not at all uncommon for a Chair to go around the boardroom to let every director "have their say" on the matter before they call the question; you want to be prepared if this occurs.

As discussed in Chapter Four, the board expects you to offer perspectives on agenda items that directly pertain to your field of expertise. For example, if you're the former Chief Information Officer of an S&P1500 company, you'd better be well-prepared to address a management request for $150 million to overhaul the company's data systems. If you're an ex-Wall Streeter, your board colleagues will expect you to lead off the questions and offer your thoughts on any capital structure issues. In fact, if you say little else at the meeting apart from addressing an agenda item directly in your wheelhouse, most people will still feel you've made a worthwhile contribution that day.

Boardroom stars add real value to the board dialogue; they judiciously inject views that are likely to have the most impact or bring a new angle to the issue at hand. Nobody expects you to change the course of a board decision with one "zinger" at every meeting. But it's not at all uncommon for directors who learn to pick their spots to receive accolades like this: "Carla only makes about three comments at every board meeting. But when Carla speaks, the whole board listens. She nearly always introduces a good point that no one else has brought up – or she asks an excellent question that hasn't yet been raised. I always find myself thinking, 'Wow! I wish I'd thought of that!' We have some directors that speak often but say very little of consequence; they could learn a lot from her example."

It almost goes without saying that the spots you need to pick should involve substantive issues and not minutiae. I once sat in a board meeting of a global conglomerate where two directors pointed out spelling mistakes and grammatical errors in the board books. Another board had to postpone their discussion of a major investment because they'd spent the first part of the meeting talking about the blueprints for the new corporate headquarters that had been included in the board pre-reading materials as an update; directors began debating whether having an exercise facility on the top floor may be noisy and distracting for those working below.

Ask the Toughest Questions in the Nicest Way

This is the hallmark of a true boardroom star – and it's worthwhile trying to cultivate this ability.

Some directors who pride themselves as "tough questioners" sound like they're cross-examining Hermann Göring at the Nuremberg trials, when in fact, they're asking the Chief Operating Officer why some cost reductions at the Minneapolis plant have yet to be realized. Not only does a harsh tone and accusatory tenor create significant boardroom tension, management can easily become defensive, distracted, and guarded. A kind of "fight or flight" response kicks in; escaping the meeting unscathed becomes the executive's foremost concern – and far more important than those cost synergies.

The Mehrabian rule suggests that over 90% of communication is non-verbal and that tone accounts for 38% of its impact, with words accounting for only 7%.[13] Some authors argue that Mehrabian's landmark UCLA study has been misinterpreted over the years.[14] But hardly anyone can deny that the tone with which a question is asked has significant impact on how it is interpreted – and on the degree of openness that characterizes the parties' discussion thereafter.

Perhaps ironically, aggressive questions often close down boardroom dialogue, with the executive becoming tense and cautious. But almost the same question, delivered in a friendly and more tactful way, can generate an open and revealing discussion, yielding better insights and information. It's hardly surprising then that one of the accolades I've repeatedly heard about directors held in high regard by their peers is that they understand the art of "asking the toughest questions in the nicest way." Three directors who have clearly developed this talent offered me some insights on their approach:

- "When I was a young executive, presenting to the board was a really big deal. I always had a little trepidation that the board was going to "trip me up". When I was nervous in a board meeting, I was never at my best. But when I relaxed – and even had fun – which happened as I became increasingly comfortable with the board, the better our conversations became. So, I try to create that sort of rapport when I'm working with management in the boardroom; I want to make them comfortable. I may have some very tough questions to ask, but I want to ask them in a way that the executive doesn't clam up and get defensive. Once that happens, the conversation hits a wall; they give you short, terse answers because they're scared. I know because I did that myself. The more comfortable you can make the Q&A in the board meeting, the more you're going to learn about the issues you're trying to get a handle on as a director."

- "We had a very significant product failure – and the executive responsible was called in front of the board to answer for it. I thought it was important to learn as much as possible about the problem: Were there any "red flags" that we might have missed? How can we make sure we don't repeat these mistakes going forward? We needed to have a very open discussion about all of this to prevent recurrence of more problems – and we wouldn't have that discussion if we made this executive feel defensive. I knew that some of my colleagues were going to pound the table over this issue; but I wanted to take a gentler approach that I felt would open up a more productive conversation."

- "I always assume positive intent on the part of the CEO and the management team. I've been on this board for five years, and they've never done anything to make me doubt that. But sometimes, things come up to the board that haven't been very well-considered; there's information missing that I would expect to see. I don't think they're trying to 'pull a fast one' when that occurs, nor do I see any point in scolding them. I just start to ask for the information, very "matter of fact". Sometimes they have it but didn't include it; who knows why. Other times they haven't thought the thing through. So, I say, "Listen, I think you've made great progress, but I can't vote on this until you address these issues. Why don't you do that and come back?"

And You Thought No One Noticed?

Executives are highly-attuned to what happens in the boardroom and how directors conduct themselves. They seldom miss a trick. Frankly, neither do most of your board colleagues:

- The Board Chair who spent time during the strategy offsite surreptitiously emailing his grandson photos of ponies as a possible birthday gift? Busted! Half the executive team was sitting right behind him; they saw every mane and tail.

- The director who spent most board meetings carefully holding his phone just beneath the board table, sending emails, texts, and checking Instagram? Busted! Directors sitting beside him finally became annoyed at his inattention and raised the matter with the Chair.

- The SOX financial expert who enjoyed a round or two of (Dare I say this? Yes, it's true!) Candy Crush on his iPad during Audit Committee meetings? Busted! Even with the distinctive music turned off, it didn't take long for the

Director of Internal Audit and others to realize what was going on.

Electronics are a fact of boardroom life. Board and committee meetings run for several hours; and every discussion has its highs and lows. It's only human nature to occasionally check your emails, glance at the latest headlines, or make sidebar comments to a colleague (although the latter is much tougher on a videoconference). But don't think that no one will notice. Boardrooms are like fishbowls.

Chapter Nine

10 COMMON BOARDROOM PITFALLS

Grandstanding

GRANDSTANDING IS ONE of the most frequent criticisms that emerges in director evaluations. It's perhaps not surprising: most boards are comprised of high-powered, successful business leaders. They're used to being in the spotlight and at the center of attention; for many, it's their comfort zone. Some directors probably consider grandstanding as entirely appropriate behavior for a boardroom star. But this tactic tends to diminish rather than enhance a director's stature.

Rather than simply making a few insightful comments or asking good questions relative to the issue at hand, some directors seem compelled to make boardroom speeches aimed at driving home their points. They often weave in some personal anecdotes to stress their expertise – and underscore the weight that should be given to their perspectives. A director who's got real passion for the company and its issues nearly always earns the respect of their peers – and of the management team – for their care, concern, and commitment. But a board member who eats up time at nearly every meeting with long-winded exhortations that appear more focused on self-aggrandizement than stakeholder interests, tends to attract more eye-rolls than genuine admiration.

Interestingly, criticisms of grandstanding are often levied at those board members with somewhat lackluster CVs in comparison to their boardroom peers. In these instances, the real issue may be insecurity. One Chair noted the following about two of his board members who'd fallen into this trap: "It's as if they feel like they have to show us all how smart they are. I know a lot of people think they're both arrogant and 'full of themselves'; I hear that all the time. But I actually perceive the real problem to be a lack of confidence. I think they behave this way because they're both rather insecure."

Taking the Board down Rabbit Holes

There's hardly a board I've worked with in the past ten years that didn't criticize at least one of their directors for routinely taking the board off-task with segues into issues that had little bearing on the agenda item under discussion. These unrelated issues are often very interesting – and directors can enjoy diving into these conversations. But the more time the board spends on the segue, the less time is available to deal with the matters on the board agenda.

Board time is precious and rabbit holes can absorb it quickly, leaving directors impatiently looking at their watches, realizing they have an hour left to cover a major investment and an update on a joint venture that isn't going well. Executives scheduled to present towards the end of the meeting have their time cut back. Afterwards, they'll nearly always tell their colleagues, "Could you believe I ended up with fifteen minutes to talk about [major issue]? You know why? I was in there for the whole meeting; they spent half an hour talking about the gym in the new headquarters building and another half hour talking about [a deal from two years ago that one director brings up at every meeting]!"

While every director can stray from the board agenda from time to time, there are some who make it a habit. Sometimes they don't have much to say on the topic under discussion, but want to say *something*, so they chime in with a comment that's pretty far afield. "Pet issues" are another problem that can cause directors to take the board off-task. Many board members have one – whether it's a new line of business they always want to focus on, a technological development that fascinates them or fallout from a major layoff last year – they'll work it into the board discussion, regardless of the actual topic at hand.

The question you should consider every time is this: Does this question or comment advance the board dialogue on the issue we're focused on or the decision the board is being asked to make? If it clearly does, it's probably an important point to raise; but if it seems like "a real stretch", you might want to reconsider. Hold your fire until the next agenda item when you have something more relevant to offer.

Waiting to Drop a Boardroom Bombshell

As you're reviewing the board materials in preparation for an upcoming meeting, you'll undoubtedly have concerns about items that the board's being asked to approve or review. Fleshing these out – so that all angles are thoroughly vetted and discussed in the meeting

– will form the basis of many of your questions and comments as you prepare.

But what if there's an issue that strikes you as a virtual non-starter – something that you feel strongly either doesn't merit board approval or that there is such important information missing with respect to this item that there is no way it should be coming before the board?

When that occurs, some directors almost rub their hands with the glee of a seasoned fisherman who just hooked "the big one" in a derby. They almost can't wait to take a stand on this issue at the meeting – pointing out in the strongest of terms that there is no way the board should be approving this matter or even considering it. This can make for some dramatic boardroom moments. But they nearly always end with the CEO and management feeling ambushed: "If you felt that way about this issue", the CEO will typically respond, "Why didn't you call and tell me that before we got into the meeting?" And most directors will wholeheartedly agree.

Giving the CEO a "head's up" about a significant concern is nearly always a better approach than dropping a boardroom bombshell mid-meeting. It gives management an opportunity to address your concerns squarely in the meeting – to come prepared to do so and to provide additional information that could make a big difference on this question. This nearly always produces a better board discussion – and ultimately a more well-informed decision. And if the proposal is truly a non-starter or simply not yet ready for the boardroom, the CEO may decide to take it off the board agenda altogether.

When a very significant concern emerges for the first time mid-meeting, the matter is often postponed to the next meeting, when management returns more fully prepared to address the evident problems – a delay that is seldom advantageous to the company. The

CEO feels blindsided, and the board often views the director who took this approach as simply grandstanding.

If directors want management to be up front in telling the board about problems between the meetings and updating them on key issues, directors need to behave similarly with the CEO. Lying in wait to drop a boardroom bombshell may seem like fun – but it can have some serious blowback.

Jumping the Gun

One of the biggest problems with board meetings in the early 2000s was that 75% of the meeting consisted of "death by PowerPoint" presentations from management, followed by board Q&A for roughly ten or fifteen minutes. This format, which largely treated the board as an audience, failed to leverage the insights and perspectives of directors and was frustrating all around.

In most S&P1500 boardrooms today, those time allocations have flipped. High performing boards insist on well-organized board materials that highlight the most important issues relative to the agenda items, followed by appropriate back-up in appendices. Management presenters are typically allocated ten or fifteen minutes at the outset of their presentation to essentially "set up" the discussion by providing an overview of the topic, highlighting the most important points. It's assumed that board members have read their materials, which is essential for this approach to work. Following the presenter's overview, a two-way dialogue or Q&A occurs with the board.

Now here's the problem: Some directors insist on "jumping the gun"; they don't give the management presenter their allocated time to set up the board dialogue properly. Before the introductory slide has flashed across the screen, they're already interrupting: "Let's cut to the chase," they'll argue, diving into some of the substantive issues relating to the item at hand.

Jumping the gun may seem like good way to create even greater meeting efficiencies. But this is seldom the case. It typically creates a lot of jumping around – a disjointed and inefficient board discussion. It's particularly frustrating for the executive, who will have worked to prepare introductory remarks covering all of the critical issues – only to have this derailed. They'll spend much of the meeting trying to get back on track, which is distracting and often counterproductive.

Unless your board is still following the old "death by PowerPoint" format where presenters drone on for half an hour or more on every item, hold your fire until the presenter has delivered their short overview – then jump in and get engaged in a terrific board discussion with all the firepower you've got.

Ignoring Management Protocols

Most boards have adopted some sort of protocol relative to directors reaching out to members of the management team below the CEO with questions or requests for information. The practice can vary from company to company:

- Some CEOs take the view that directors can reach out to anyone in management at any time to discuss anything they wish. They don't even need to notify the CEO when they do so.

- Other CEOs have a very different view. They ask that board members raise their questions with the CEO first, before contacting anyone in management. "Most of the time, I'll know the answer," CEOs who have adopted this practice typically explain, "If I can't answer the question, I can tell them who to call and I'll let that person know, so that they're expecting to hear from someone on the board and won't be taken aback by an outreach from a director."

- Yet others have adopted a sort of "middle ground" approach: A director can email anyone in management with questions or information requests but are asked to copy the CEO on their correspondence. CEOs who favor this practice often do so for these reasons: "If an employee hears from a board member, they can become concerned or intimidated. They wonder what it's all about – and nearly always come to me straightaway and ask what to do. If I haven't been copied on the director's request, it creates some awkwardness as I may not know, myself. But if they see that I've been copied, they'll usually just go ahead and respond. If I think the director's reached out to the wrong person or hasn't been clear in what they're looking for, I can also intervene to curtail any misunderstandings or miscommunication."

Interactions between a board committee chair and the executive liaison who supports the committee's work are typically excluded from this standard protocol; they connect on a regular basis without any need to inform the CEO regardless of the protocol. In most cases, this practice extends to other committee members working with the executive liaison as well. Otherwise, the board/management protocol, whatever it may be, generally applies to all director outreaches to management.

As a board member, it's important to follow the protocol on board/management interactions. Even if you're frustrated by the response – or lack of response – that you're getting to your questions or requests, an end-run is rarely a good idea. One director, who was called out for this in front of the entire board by the CEO, was left red-faced from the experience. Another got some tough feedback from her peers on this issue in her director evaluation, where she was criticized for her "bad judgment" in making it appear that "the board is trying to dig up dirt on the CEO." This was not her intent; she was merely curious about some important issues. But this approach reflected negatively on her.

If you're not getting the information you've asked for or feel that you need better responses than management's providing, take the issue up with the Lead Director, the Chair, or the CEO. If you believe that the management protocol itself should be changed, raise that issue in an executive session. Circumventing the process seldom ends well.

Overwhelming Information Requests

A very different but not unrelated issue involves inordinate board requests for additional information made during the board meetings. This is one of the biggest complaints I hear from CEOs and senior management: nearly everything that any director asks for in the course of a board meeting finds its way onto a "To Do" list, frequently requiring hours or even days of management time to recalculate, modify, and furnish the information requested. The Chair or Lead Director, who should serve as a filter in this regard – determining which requests are essential and which are simply not worth the time and effort – seldom plays this role in practice.

Many director requests are entirely reasonable – sometimes, in fact, the information is so essential that one might consider management almost negligent in coming to the board without it. But other requests seem inspired by nothing more than director musings,

"Hmmm ... I wonder what the financials would look like if we got a 20% market share in the first nine months instead of just 5%, as we're anticipating?"

Fortune 500 companies with virtual armies of administrative staff can absorb board requests far more readily than midcaps and smallcaps, which have limited resources that they often resent having to divert from "more important work" to respond to a board member's question. But regardless of the organization's size, overwhelming information requests from the board reflect scant regard for management's time and priorities.

Whenever you're going to ask management for some follow up information in a board meeting, it's important to consider how important the information really is: If it's essential – if it can make a real difference to the board's decision or to directors' understanding of the magnitude of a significant risk – your request is non-negotiable. But if it's far more of a "nice to have" than a "must have", to help you determine whether to ask for the information or not, it can be useful to ask the CEO – or the executive making the presentation – whether it would take very long to recalculate or develop the information you'd like to see. If they say, "Oh, that's easy; less than five minutes"– ask away! If instead, you're told that it would require three people in the marketing department about two days to rebuild the entire model, you need to determine if it's worth that level of management resources to provide your answer.

Either way, they'll appreciate the fact that you asked. And by doing so, you might even start a trend: other directors may follow your lead and a pervasive management frustration throughout the S&P1500 may all but vanish from your boardroom.

Boardroom Confidentiality

Most directors are scrupulous about boardroom confidentiality – observing the utmost discretion even with their spouse or partner. Breaches of board confidentiality are rare; of nearly 200 boards that I've worked with over the past 25 years, I only heard about this sort of problem on five occasions. Yet even those five instances struck me – and the other board members involved in them – as "way too many".

Two of these instances were pretty blatant: In one case, a director had "leaked" information to a reporter; in another, a director had given information to a private equity firm in order to interest them in the company as a potential investment or acquisition. In the latter case, the board member had acted entirely on his own – and shared confidential information with the firm. However well-intentioned his outreach (and he insisted that it was), it nonetheless ended with his resignation from the board.

The other three were more nuanced. Two involved confidential information shared with the former CEO; the third, a similar indiscretion with a former C-suite executive. This is an easy trap to fall into. After all, board members typically form good working relationships with the CEO and others in senior management. Friendships begun in the boardroom often continue for years after the executive retires or departs, particularly if they leave on good terms. It's not at all uncommon for a director to go out for a drink, dinner, or a round of golf with the former CEO, during which the latter might quite naturally ask, "So, how are things going at the old shop? What are the big issues they're working on now?"

And before you know it …

The One-Note Director

"I can tell you exactly what each of my directors is going to say about every issue on the board agenda," a CEO once bragged. "Bruce is going to talk about costs; when are we finally going to get our costs under control? That's his shtick; no matter how much we've reduced the costs in some division, Bruce will always suggest that there's still more 'fat to trim'. Laura is going to talk about innovation and new ideas – how we're always just doing the 'same old, same old'; she says this in every meeting, and she always brings up some funky new technology she just read about and goes off on a tangent about it. Colin's a deal guy; he's always saying that we're not doing enough M&A transactions; we could do six deals and stretch our management team to the breaking point, and it would never be enough for Colin. Listen, these are actually all great issues to raise, I'm not knocking any of them. But here's my point: My directors only play one note. They talk about the same thing and make the same point every time."

It's not uncommon for directors to focus in an area where they have expertise, passion, and real concern. But when any director's remarks become too predictable, they begin to carry less weight; it seems that this board member raises "the same thing at every meeting". Even well-considered and important comments can lose their impact when a director has adopted this tendency.

Let's be clear: This is not about a director with a legal background who routinely weighs in on legal issues; that's expected – and when it happens, the director will typically voice a positive view about one lawsuit and a negative view on another legal matter. A one-note director, by contrast, lacks balance in their comments; they're nearly always skewed in the same way. A classic example is the boardroom curmudgeon. Many directors slip into this role and rather pride themselves on being "the devil's advocate" or the "nay-sayer" of the boardroom. But over time, their boardroom peers and even the executive team start to shrug off their negative comments, which have become "routine", like the boy who cried wolf.

It's easy to become a "one-note director" and a trap that you'd do well to avoid. If you find yourself becoming the cynic of the boardroom; find something positive to extoll. If you're the boardroom cheerleader, point out some downsides or risks on an important matter. If you keep "pounding away" at a particular issue, give it a rest; your perspectives are likely to carry more weight when you revisit them later on. Seek to broaden your lens and balance your comments to avoid this common pitfall.

CEO Lapdogs

CEO lapdogs treat the Chief Executive deferentially, support almost everything management wants to do and pepper their boardroom remarks with almost cringe-worthy adulation. I can't think of a single director regarded by their peers as a CEO lapdog who was also considered a boardroom star. "Lapdog" is one of the kinder terms I've heard used to describe this pitfall; you can only imagine some of the others.

Acknowledging your CEO's achievements, praising their progress, and supporting them through tough times is something any good director should do. Boards that don't express appreciation to their CEO and senior executives for "a job well done" are wasting an important opportunity; few comments mean more to corporate brass than a sincere and well-deserved compliment from the boardroom for their efforts. One CEO, who'd steered his company through the financial crisis of 2008–9, recalled one of his most thrilling boardroom moments nearly ten years later: "They gave me a standing ovation. My board! They stood up and applauded for me and my senior team for all we'd done to navigate these problems. How many CEOs have ever had that happen? It meant the world to me!"

But directors who become CEO sycophants impair their credibility with boardroom peers. Even management tends to discount their fawning. They are often excluded from any off-line director conversations where criticism is expressed about the CEO's performance, integrity, or similar matters. Not only do their fellow directors believe their concerns about the CEO will fall on "deaf ears", they worry that the lapdog may "run to the CEO" with their comments in a further effort to curry favor.

Undermining Board Decisions

An issue has emerged that you feel strongly about – and you've made the case that supporting this management proposal would be a big mistake. Notwithstanding your eloquence and excellent points, the board has approved it. You're undoubtedly concerned and likely a bit disheartened. There's only one thing to do: support the board's decision – even if you personally held a different view.

A great example of this involved a director I'll call Bob, a prominent member of the community where the company had been headquartered for more than fifty years. Recruiting new and tech-savvy talent had become big problem over the past ten years – and the new CEO had decided to solve it: corporate headquarters would move to the suburb of a major city in the same state, leaving a field office behind that would continue to employ more than four hundred people in the local community.

Intense board debate on this topic emerged – and no one was more vehemently opposed to this idea than Bob, who made an eloquent case and raised many important considerations. But after three animated meetings, the board held a vote – and approved the headquarters move.

Bob couldn't let the issue go. When he raised it again at the next meeting and the meeting after that – vehemently expressing his disapproval and repeating the points he'd made earlier, directors listened patiently. They knew it was a tough decision for Bob to accept. And they realized he'd be getting an earful from the town council, his friends at the local golf club, and his neighbors at the grocery store. It wasn't an easy position for him to be in.

But before long, gossip filtered back about how Bob was handling those comments – with blistering remarks about his "short-sighted" board colleagues, their "stupid mistake" and the company's "incompetent new CEO". Bob, himself, continued to raise the issue at subsequent board meetings – and then he went even further: he brought it up endlessly with other members of management – in conversations at board dinners, elevator chats on the way to meetings, phone calls to executives he knew well – all aimed at trying to "get some dirt" on emerging problems relative to the new headquarters so that he could attempt to reopen the issue with the board. By doing so, Bob had become a "problem director". The new CEO began to advocate for a board retirement age, which everyone realized was nothing more than a device to rid the board of Bob, who was 73. And while most felt that this tactic was "far too harsh", others started to think that Bob "had to go".

Governance is a team sport. Your job as a board member is to advocate for the position you believe is in the company's best interests and that of its key stakeholders; raise all the points that you feel have a bearing on the question and outline your thinking around each. But if the board, as a whole, reaches a different conclusion than the one you think is correct, there are only two options: If it's a decision that you just can't live with, you can resign from the board – and you should. If you choose to remain on the board, you need to support the board's decision, regardless of your personal view on the matter. To do otherwise, undermines the board's authority and will ultimately reflect poorly on you.

Chapter Ten

PROFILES IN BOARDROOM COURAGE

COURAGE IS ONE of the defining features of a boardroom star. There are typically one or two key moments in nearly every director's board career where they face a decision that requires courage. This chapter describes four boardroom stars who rose to very different challenges – and did the right thing, earning the respect of their peers and the satisfaction of knowing that they acted with integrity, putting the best interests of the company and its stakeholders at the foreground of their decisions.

A New Director Offers a Contrary View – That Makes a Big Difference

Trevor had joined the board of a Fortune 500 company just over a year ago – his first board seat. He was the young, tech-savvy director who was purposefully recruited to offer a different perspective from that of the "the old guard" and expected to weigh in on technology issues, which formed an increasingly important facet of the company's strategy. Trevor was in his mid-40s and still working as a top executive at a Silicon Valley firm. He had aspirations to become a CEO someday and felt that serving on one external board would help him get a feel for being "on the other side of the board table."

This board's make-up included two extremely well-regarded former CEOs, who were routinely interviewed by the *Wall Street Journal* on a range of business issues and asked to keynote various conferences since their retirement. The board held them both in very high regard; Trevor, himself, was thrilled to be serving on a board where he could watch directors of this caliber in action and learned a great deal from that experience. It didn't take long for Trevor to notice, however, that once these two directors weighed in on an issue – and they generally held the same view – none of the other directors would offer a contrary perspective. This had clearly become a boardroom norm. And in fairness, these two board members were nearly always right; Trevor himself seldom disagreed with their perspectives.

Until one day – when an item emerged on the board agenda that involved a technology issue. It was more of an update at this point than a matter that required board approval and Trevor had given the issue a lot of thought. He'd formed a pretty definitive view that, despite some risks involved in venturing into this new direction, it presented a unique opportunity that was worth some pretty serious consideration – and investment. Shortly into the board discussion, however, the two former CEOs weighed in: they, too, had thought about this issue and felt it was simply too far afield; the company should "stick to its knitting". Other board members nodded in agreement; one even made a joke about how "off the radar" this "kooky idea" seemed to be.

"It was tempting," Trevor recalled, "to just let it go. It wasn't a really big deal. But it was a unique opportunity for the company. I just didn't think we should dismiss it out of hand." So, Trevor spoke up. He began his remarks by telling the board, "Well, you guys said when you recruited me that you hoped I'd offer a different perspective at times. I'd like to do so on this issue. I hope you'll hear me out." He then went on to explain why he felt there was real potential in this new idea, how some of the apparent risks could be easily overcome and that he'd encourage the board to keep an open mind on the issue. "When I finished, you could hear a pin drop," Trevor recalled, "In fact, people were averting their eyes. The Chair thanked me for my remarks and moved on."

However, when the same matter returned to the board agenda two meetings later – this time for a funding request – the board had changed its tune; the investment was approved. The Chair went around the room and said, "Trevor, I know you expressed your views on this last time, do you have anything to add?" He did not – and no one said another word to Trevor about the matter.

But a few months later, the board undertook a director evaluation process. I was engaged to interview every director to provide some constructive feedback for their peers. And Trevor was blown away by the comments in his evaluation report: Almost to a person, the board expressed their admiration for Trevor's willingness to offer a contrary perspective on the issue where he "went against the grain", applauded his courage, and commended the gracious way he had handled the matter: "He acknowledged that he had a different point of view – but he didn't make other people 'wrong'." "He shared his perspective, and we all respected him for it." "He raised points that no one else had considered – and it made the board rethink the whole thing."

Interestingly, the most complimentary of all were the two well-regarded CEOs whose perspective Trevor had challenged. One of them told me: "It was so refreshing to have somebody on the board say, 'You know what, I don't agree with you on this one. Here's why.' Quite frankly, the other directors don't challenge Ed and I enough. We nearly always come to the same conclusion on a lot of issues, but we're not always right! I think we knew when we recruited Trevor that he was going to be a terrific director even though he was young and inexperienced – and it seems we were right about that!"

A Nominating/Governance Committee Chair Makes Some Tough Decisions

Kate had never been the Chair of a Nominating and Governance Committee before – and she took the role seriously. The board was already bloated at sixteen directors, several of whom routinely came to meetings unprepared and said little. "From what I understood," Kate explained, "as the Nominating and Governance Committee Chair, I had a role in making sure we had the right board composition – and in ensuring that our board was operating effectively. Our board was far too big, and we kept re-nominating people who weren't adding any value to the board whatsoever."

Kate began by creating a set of Director Expectations – and engaged every member of the board and the CEO in this exercise: "I didn't want this to be Kate's idea of what was expected of board members; everybody needed to weigh in and buy in." Sample Director Expectations are found at Appendix C-1, although these were adapted from another board, not Kate's. Once the Director Expectations were developed, reviewed, and approved by the board, Kate put them on the company's website. "Frankly," she joked, "I don't think anyone ever thought they'd see them again. But they did!"

Nine months later, when the time came to re-nominate board members, Kate brought out the Director Expectations. The board was too large, she told her committee, and she suggested that the Expectations should be a factor in the committee's re-nomination decisions. "It made for a tough committee meeting – and some rather emotional discussion. But in the end, we reached a unanimous agreement: There were two directors who barely spoke in the meetings and another who never came prepared and often left early. We concluded that none of these directors should be re-nominated."

The following year, I had the pleasure of working with Kate when she engaged me to conduct a director evaluation for her board: "I wanted to go further this time," she explained, "I wanted to have an outsider interview everyone and give people really constructive feedback that they'd find helpful for professional development. My job as Chair of the Nominating and Governance Committee is to make the board as effective as possible – and I think this can help build the board into a better team."

"But I can only imagine what you'll hear about me," she said with a smile, "I'll get some horrific feedback for getting rid of those three directors last year. I was a heartless shrew who destroyed board collegiality! And that's ok; I did what I felt was the right thing to do. I think our board is better now that we're a bit smaller and without those three people who honestly weren't adding any value."

Kate could not have been more wrong. Her fellow directors extolled her courage in stepping up to a tough issue and making some difficult choices that nearly all felt "had to be made". "We all knew the board was too big, and we had some directors who weren't contributing at all," one board member told me, "But our last Nominating and Governance Chair just turned a blind eye to it; he didn't want to get his hands dirty. That's one of the reasons Kate was such a good choice; she's fearless! And she used a process, which I think was brilliant. She created director expectations first; now she's using director evaluations – everybody gets to weigh in. If she hadn't done something like this, I think people could easily have said, 'Kate's just getting rid of people she doesn't like.' But she was fair about the process, and she absolutely did the right thing in terms of the decisions that were made."

A Compensation Committee Chair Holds the Line

Rosemary became Chair of the Compensation Committee of a company that had an outstanding CEO – one who was extremely well-paid for his accomplishments. The board had never been entirely comfortable with the size of the bonuses routinely recommended by the previous committee chair, but they were always approved; the company's performance had been stellar, and the stockholders had no complaints, even if the bonuses and equity grants seemed a little "stratospheric" compared to those awarded to other CEOs in the company's peer group.

But in Rosemary's very first year as committee chair, things went south. The entire industry began shifting. Although the company was weathering the storm somewhat better than others, its stock price had dropped substantially, and two strategic initiatives once considered "game-changing" had been mothballed. In the circumstances, Rosemary could hardly justify giving the CEO the type of bonus and equity grants he'd become accustomed to.

Before the first meeting to consider the CEO's annual bonus, the Chief Human Resources Officer told Rosemary that she should be aware that the CEO's "expectations remain unchanged in terms of his compensation level". Clearly this was a shot across the bow. The compensation consultants laid out the options, calculated the award that would likely result from the bonus formula but pointed out that the committee had discretion to "sweeten" the total compensation package in a number of different ways. The very formula that had yielded such high payouts in the past, swung back hard in the other direction when times were tough and the CEO's total compensation level was drastically reduced.

Rosemary wasn't comfortable with the proposed "sweeteners": "This has been a rough year – and we need to reflect that" she told the committee, whereupon the CHRO and one of the committee members immediately challenged her: "The CEO has been under tremendous pressure this year – more than ever before. We need to find a way to acknowledge his efforts and show our appreciation for all he's done. He's the reason our stock hasn't tanked even more!" Rosemary suggested that the committee reconvene on this issue; final results for the year weren't yet in and the initial estimate was only preliminary. However, they had a sense of where things were likely to end up.

Next day, Rosemary received a call from the CEO. He told her that he understood her conundrum. He'd agree to a minimal decrease "for the sake of shareholder optics" and threw out a total compensation number for the year that he'd consider "acceptable". Rosemary told the CEO that his expectations were unrealistic. She threw out a number that she considered acceptable. He hung up.

In the weeks that followed, Rosemary fielded calls from other directors and the former Chair of the Compensation Committee, a director named Leo, who had since retired. All of them warned that the CEO was threatening to resign if his compensation expectations weren't met. Rosemary replied that his expectations were unreasonable – and that the board would be pilloried in the business press and at the next Annual Meeting by acceding to his wishes.

Then a call came in from the third member of the compensation committee. Jeff had been the CEO of a larger company – and he was the person the board planned to name Interim CEO in a "hit by a bus" scenario. Jeff told Rosemary that he supported her 100% in holding the line against the CEO's "childish and petulant behavior". "He was used to bullying Leo," Jeff told Rosemary, "And Leo was afraid of him. But you're not. And I'll back you to the wall. If he quits, I'm happy to step in and run the company until we replace him; we'll survive. And if the board doesn't support your recommendation on his pay and votes to give him what he wants, I plan to resign from the board. I expect you probably will, too. I really admire you for having the guts to stand up to him."

The committee voted two to one to recommend a low bonus with a very modest adjustment; it was significantly below the CEO's demands. The board meeting the next day began with an executive session to discuss the matter. With the CEO out of the room, Jeff made the case for the committee's decision right after Rosemary presented it: "It's the right thing to do – and I think you all know it. He's making a lot of threats and he could follow through on them, but I suspect he won't. If you back our committee's pay recommendation and he quits, I'll step in if you like until we find a permanent replacement. If you vote our pay recommendation down, I plan to resign. I don't want to be on any board that agrees to a package like the one he's demanding when the stock's been in freefall for much of the year."

The board voted to support the committee's recommendation. The CEO didn't resign. In fact, he told Rosemary two years later, "I'll admit, you were hardly my favorite person at the time. But I respected you for taking a stand – and I have ever since."

A Lead Director Admits a Mistake

It takes courage to admit that you made a mistake. Especially when you're the Lead Director. Ken, the Lead Director of a midcap S&P1500 company, had been friends for many years with Mark, the retiring CEO of a large organization in the Pacific Northwest. When Mark announced his intention to retire, Ken lobbied his Nominating and Governance Committee to consider recruiting Mark to their board.

The board wasn't actively looking for a new director. Had they been, the committee would have prioritized someone with a current industry background, who might serve to further diversify the board's composition. The committee chair was initially resistant to Ken's overtures but finally agreed to meet with Mark when Ken pointed out that, "It's not every day you have an opportunity to recruit a Fortune 500 CEO – and Mark used to be a CFO, so he can also chair the Audit Committee. He even led a major technology initiative at his own company."

Mark was impressive. And the rest of the committee agreed that he had a lot to offer as a director. They recommended his appointment to the board and the motion passed unanimously.

Mark refused to attend director orientation. He told the Nominating and Governance Committee that he was "a quick study" and didn't have time. It was evident that he hadn't read the materials for the first board meeting he attended; his questions largely related to items that were covered in-depth in the board books and in most cases, the executive summaries. He spent most of the board meeting with his head down, looking at emails or skimming news items on his iPhone.

Ken was embarrassed; his would-be boardroom star had failed to shine. After a repeat performance at the next meeting, Ken had a conversation with Mark. "Listen, I went to bat to get you onto this board," he told Mark, "But it's clear that you're not putting in any effort here. I'm disappointed, Mark, because you have so much to contribute."

Mark's response astonished him: "Listen, I came on this board as a favor to you, Ken. My joining this board gave the company some cachet with the Street. What am I even doing on this board?! This company's much smaller than the one I used to run and it's not exactly in an exciting line of business. Just by putting my name on the proxy, as far as I'm concerned, I've done my bit."

Needless to say, little changed at the next two meetings. During one of them, Mark left the boardroom for more than half an hour, chatting on his phone out in the hallway, engaged in what appeared to be a social conversation. He also informed the Nominating and Governance Committee Chair that he didn't have time to serve on any of the board committees, especially Audit; he was sure she'd understand.

That's when Ken stepped up and addressed the situation: he told the CEO and the Nominating and Governance Committee Chair that he'd made a mistake in recommending Mark. He'd created an awkward situation for the board, and he'd resolve it, even if it meant that his friendship with Mark might suffer. They all agreed that Mark had been a tremendous disappointment. His "marquee name status" was of little importance, although they recognized that Mark's coming on and off the board in quick succession might raise some Wall Street eyebrows. But it was in the board's best interest for Mark to be replaced – and they already had some good ideas about other candidates.

Ken made good on his promise. He told Mark, "I thought a lot about what you said. And I appreciate your coming on the board as a favor to me. But it's not a good use of your time or your talent, Mark. I've spoken to the Nominating and Governance Committee Chair; if you want to tender your resignation, they'll accept it. In fact, they want to recruit a new director anyway, so I think it will all work out for the best for everyone. It keeps the board from getting too big."

Mark was startled. He certainly didn't expect this response. He attempted to backtrack – and pointed out the potential "optics issue" if he left the board so soon. But Ken was having none of it. "I spoke to the CEO about that – but we're not concerned. We appreciate your being forthright about the whole situation and we want to do the right thing. The right thing is for you to have the freedom to go on another board more in keeping with your stature." Mark submitted his resignation later that evening.

"It takes a real leader to admit you've made a mistake," the Nominating/Governance Chair told Ken when he gave her an update. "I'm on another board where our Chair recommended a director who's far more of a headache than Mark ever was. But the Chair's completely entrenched in supporting this guy, even though he's a nightmare. He doesn't have the courage to admit he was wrong – or to deal with the problem. I know you were embarrassed when Mark didn't pan out; but you stepped up, acknowledged the problem, and resolved the situation. That's leadership."

PART IV
Board Leadership

Chapter Eleven

A BOARDROOM STAR BECOMES A BOARDROOM CHAMPION

AS DISCUSSED IN Chapter Two, a boardroom star is a director who:

i. makes valuable contributions to board dialogue by asking critical questions and offering important insights and perspectives on the issues the board is dealing with; *and*

ii. plays a key role in supporting and advancing the effectiveness of the board as a team.

Not surprisingly, boardroom stars are nearly always asked to assume board leadership roles, typically as a committee chair at the outset; later on, they are often appointed as the leader of the independent directors, be that Non-Executive Board Chair or Lead Director.

Upon assuming a board leadership role – even if this only involves chairing an "ad hoc" board committee – a boardroom star has an opportunity to become a boardroom champion. I define a boardroom champion as someone in a board leadership position who has a genuine commitment to excellence. Champions want to ensure that their committee and/or the board itself is truly performing at the top of its game. If their fellow directors sit on other boards, they want them to say, referencing the board (or committee) the champion leads, "*That's* the best board I'm on!"

Boardroom champions want to lead the kind of board/committee that stakeholders would be genuinely proud to have representing their interests – one that has vibrant meetings, raises fresh perspectives, thoroughly vets critical issues, and makes good decisions. They want to build constructive working relationships with management, in which the board/committee adds real value for the executive team, holds management accountable, and where executives walk out of meetings saying "Wow!" – maybe not every meeting, but it's important to any champion that the board/committee they lead genuinely earns management's respect.

Champions recognize that boards are teams – and teams tend to do their best work in an energized environment. The climate of a champion's boardroom or committee meeting is characterized by openness and candor; there's a good "give and take" amongst directors themselves and between the board and management. Important points and critical issues emerge to stimulate a great discussion; people genuinely care about making the right decision and want to ensure they've examined all sides of the question. Meetings, at times, are downright fun – because boardroom champions bring out the best in their directors, leveraging their expertise, talents, and insights.

One of the hallmarks of a boardroom champion is a commitment to continuous improvement. They constantly look for opportunities to make their board/committee even better, regardless of how well it's performing today. Not only do they keep abreast of latest developments, ideas, and best practices, they actively solicit worthwhile and actionable feedback about the board/committee and about their own leadership. They're not afraid of feedback; they see it as an essential tool to achieving and maintaining excellence. Nor are they afraid to give feedback – both well-deserved praise and, when appropriate, calling out performance that misses the mark, a thorny issue that we'll explore in Chapter Fourteen.

Champions and Preservationists

One of the most prominent shareholder activists in America once asked me:

> Do you know what the real difference is between the board of a private equity firm and the board of a public company? I'll tell you. When you're on the board of a private equity firm, much of your wealth and your family's future and security is directly impacted by the decisions that you're going make in that board meeting. So, you need to listen carefully, think critically, bring all your intellect and all your expertise to bear to make the best possible decisions you can, in order to increase the value of your investments. That's your job as a board member of a private equity firm.
>
> Do you know what job is of a board member of a public company? To do everything possible to stay on the board.

Although his remark was somewhat facetious, it holds a kernel of truth, even today. Despite all the changes boards have undergone since the demise of Enron twenty years ago, there are still some people who serve on boards largely for prestige and, to a lesser extent, for income. They're comfortable just the way things are – and have a vested interest in keeping them that way. Collegiality is their watchword – and their excuse for refusing to tackle issues of director performance, CEO incompetence, and strategic misfires. They seldom become boardroom stars. If they take on a board leadership position, they're never champions. I call them preservationists.

Boardroom preservationists are largely motivated by status, and they want to maintain the status quo. They'll go to extraordinary lengths to extend their board tenure and protect any board leadership position they've managed to secure. Most preservationists will proudly nod at well-crafted Governance Guidelines, trumpeting the board's commitment to stewardship and good governance. But true boardroom excellence – all the things a champion seeks to achieve – never drives a preservationist. Boardroom mediocrity is just fine with them; in fact, it's pretty much perfect, from their perspective. Excellence can be threatening.

Preservationist directors are far fewer in number than they used to be. Moreover, they ascend to Board Chair or Lead Director roles less frequently because their boardroom peers recognize their lack of leadership and find ways to thwart their boardroom ambitions. But some of them do manage it. Most of the boards they lead are fairly lackluster. However, it's possible to have a preservationist Chair and a champion Nominating and Governance Committee Chair, who leverages their responsibilities for board composition and evaluation to take that board from good to great. It's also possible to have the reverse, a champion Chair who drags the Nominating and Governance Committee – and the rest of the board for that matter – into twenty-first century governance. Not every board leader needs to be a champion to create an outstanding board.

Becoming a boardroom champion gives you an opportunity to expand your boardroom influence – and to play a role in building and maintaining a board that serves as a beacon of excellence at the top of the organization it governs. I hope you'll rise to that challenge - and that these chapters will be helpful to you in doing so.

Chapter Twelve

BECOMING A BOARD COMMITTEE CHAIR

YOUR FIRST BOARD leadership role will typically involve chairing a board committee: Audit, HR/Compensation, Nominating/Governance, Finance, Technology, or something else. Much of the board's important work is done in committees and the committee chair's effectiveness plays a significant role in optimizing the committee's performance in fulfilling its mandate.

A committee chair role is also an opportunity to demonstrate your capacity for more significant board leadership roles in the future, potentially that of Chair or Lead Director. Few US boards would consider "recruiting in" a Board Chair from the outside – a practice that's not at all uncommon in the UK and other countries. North American boards nearly always choose their Non-Executive Chair or Lead Director from among their current board membership, selecting someone they feel has shown good capabilities in running committee meetings and in working with the CEO and fellow directors.

Preliminary One-on-Ones: Committee Members

It's a common practice for a director to have served as a committee member prior to becoming committee chair; this typically makes for a more seamless transition of committee leadership. If you've already been a member of the committee you're now chairing, you'll undoubtedly have formed some views as to where the committee's working well and where there might be opportunities for further improvement. But before you set about putting any changes into motion, you might do well to gather some additional feedback from the other committee members and even the former chair.

This can involve nothing more than some informal videoconference calls. These not only build rapport, they can provide terrific insights. Here are some questions you might consider asking:

- What do you see as the strengths of our committee? What does the committee do particularly well, in your opinion? What did you see as the strengths of the prior chair in leading the committee – practices that I'd do well to continue during my tenure as chair?

- If you were going to change just one or two things about our committee that you think would make it even more effective, what would you change – and why?

- What are your thoughts on the structure of the committee agenda? Is there anything you think we should talk about that hasn't been on the agenda for a while? What about the committee pre-reading materials? Can these be improved in any way?

- Do you have any comments about [name of executive liaison who supports the committee's work] – what do you see as their strengths?

- What about our [external resource that supports the committee work, such as a compensation consultant]?

- Do you have any other comments or advice for me as the new committee chair?

These conversations may well confirm your own views – or they might surface issues you hadn't even considered. They won't take long and are nearly always worthwhile. They serve as your first step in keeping "a finger on the pulse" of your committee, something you'll want to do throughout your chairmanship to make sure that you and your committee members are largely on the same page.

Executive Liaison

A preliminary conversation with your executive liaison is also essential at the outset of your chairmanship. Ask about the pattern of their working relationship with the prior chair: who took the "first cut" at the committee agenda, when did the chair and the executive liaison connect prior to and after the meetings? Determine if you want to adopt the same meeting cadence as your predecessor – or make some changes that you think might work better.

Ask the executive liaison for their views on the committee's strengths – and where they believe further enhancements could be made. It can also be worthwhile to get their take on any external advisors who support the committee's work.

External Advisors

It's also important to have a preliminary discussion with external advisors who regularly support the committee's work, such as auditors or compensation consultants. These conversations can be particularly enlightening because external advisors have experience working with many different boards – and therefore can offer a perspective on how your committee compares. Because you're new in the chair's role, they can be honest if they think there's room for improvement; some might not be as candid with a longer-serving chair, as they might be seen as criticizing the chair's leadership. By exploring this question early on, they're likely to give you some unvarnished feedback and some good ideas.

They can also network you to other clients – directors who chair the same committee on other boards; these can be valuable connections. For example, it's not a bad idea to have another Compensation Committee Chair or two who you reach out to for a discussion on an emerging issue in CEO pay. External advisors can also be a good source of insights about resources in their field; they'll tell you which journals they consider the most worthwhile and which conferences they'd recommend, all of which can help you keep up to date and make the best use of your time.

Committee Materials and Agendas

Of nearly 200 board evaluations I've conducted over the past 25 years, roughly two-thirds identified board and committee materials as an area for improvement. There's a good chance that your committee materials could be streamlined or better organized, as well. These changes shouldn't be that tough to introduce with the assistance of your executive liaison. If your preliminary conversations suggest that committee members are somewhat frustrated in this regard, tackle this issue right at the outset; you'll create "raving fans", and your committee meetings will be far more effective.

Committee agendas are another mundane topic that can make a big difference. Some agendas have become so rote that it appears almost as if the committee's been having the same meeting since 2013. Consider ways to refresh the committee agenda. Even minor adjustments to the way the committee spends its time can reinvigorate committee meetings and make them more productive.

Meeting Facilitation

Meeting facilitation lies at the heart of effective board leadership. An effective leader has the ability to chair a lively meeting that generates terrific exchanges, injects fresh perspectives, remains at a governance/oversight level, stays on topic, and reaches consensus. Not all chairs understand this art.

Throughout the board meeting, it's important for the chair's head to be up, not down – watching the body language amongst participants; not taking notes or preparing for the next agenda item. A gifted chair looks for opportunities to "draw in" the quieter members to express their views and intervenes to curtail off-topic segues, repetitive comments, and micro-management. They work hard to bring out all the angles and perspectives that relate to the question under consideration and guide the committee to reach a consensus decision on the issue. They provide clear direction to management or to their advisors, so that there's no ambiguity about what the committee has decided upon as next steps.

Some chairs believe that they shouldn't weigh in on the issues; they see their primary role as facilitating the discussion. That's not true. The committee (and the board, in the case of the Board

Chair) benefits from the chair's perspective. However, an effective chair never dominates the meeting nor tries to pilot the discussion towards their own point of view. Some chairs deliberately wait to express their opinions until later in the dialogue so that others can weigh in without being influenced by the chair's perspective.

Committee Updates to the Board

Many board meetings start with reports from their committee chairs, updating non-committee members about the committee's activities and decisions. This is often the dullest component of any board meeting; some committee chairs end up reading notes prepared by their executive liaison.

There's a range of practices when it comes to the board/committee interface: Some boards direct non-committee members to the minutes of committee meetings; others almost rehash the entire committee meeting in the full board. Neither works well. A board committee chair should give a succinct summary of what the committee's working on and the decisions it's reached, including the key considerations that went into that decision. Unless it's a very controversial issue or a recommendation for a board vote, this shouldn't take much more than ten minutes.

The Compensation Committee is generally the most controversial; executive pay has been a lightning rod in the media and shareholder activist community for decades. Some Compensation Committee chairs host a meeting once a year for all directors that provides an overview of the committee's compensation philosophy, peer group analysis, bonus, and equity programs, etc.; the board's compensation consultants and the CHRO take part in this presentation. It provides every member of the board with a foundation on this topic;

when the committee chair provides updates at board meetings thereafter, directors have more context for the committee's decisions.

There's no reason other committee chairs couldn't consider a similar approach if they find they're getting an inordinate number of questions from fellow directors in their committee updates. Directors' newfound comfort with videoconferencing means that these updates could be scheduled at almost any time, rather than incorporated into a board agenda, and attendance could be optional.

Chapter Thirteen

KEY FACETS OF THE BOARD CHAIR'S ROLE

KEY FACETS OF the Board Chair's role outlined in this chapter apply to the role of a Lead Director as well, with one important exception: the Lead Director doesn't facilitate the board meetings apart from executive sessions. Interestingly, however, I've recently seen two instances where a Chair/CEO asked their Lead Director to facilitate a particularly important segment of a board meeting: in one instance a major acquisition, in another, a strategic issue. This was done so the CEO could "play hard" as a member of management, rather than having to focus on facilitating the board discussion.

Practically speaking, the Board Chair role is very similar to that of a committee chair, as discussed in Chapter Twelve, on an expanded scale. If you take on the Chair role, you'll be leading a much larger group – the full board, rather than a relatively small committee. Instead of an executive liaison, you'll be working with the CEO.

You'll need to keep a finger on the pulse of the board, just as you would by checking in with your committee members regularly. But because the board is larger and has a broader range of issues to deal with, this requires far more time and effort. Board Chairs typically spend a significant amount of time in discussions with their committee chairs between meetings, given the importance of the committees' work.

Some Chairs take on an ambassadorial role on behalf of the board, representing the company at community, industry, and employee events. This could also involve meetings with key investors. One could argue that every director serves as an ambassador of the board and of the company, which is true, but the Chair and/or Lead Director title carries even more weight in this regard. The role of the Chair and/or Lead Director is also more important in terms of setting the "tone at the top", not only for the board, but for the entire organization.

If you're new to the role of Chair or Lead Director, it can be useful to start with the same type of preliminary one-on-one discussions outlined in Chapter Twelve, this time with every member of the board, to gauge their sense of the board's effectiveness, strengths, and areas for potential improvement. Determine whether board members want to work with you somewhat differently than they did with your predecessor – and understand their perceptions of what the prior Chair did well, so that you can continue those practices. You'll likely have your own ideas in this regard, as well, but it can nonetheless be useful to gather the views of the other directors on this question.

You should have a preliminary conversation with the Chief Executive Officer similar to that which you'd have with your executive liaison as a committee chair. Determine the cadence of your meetings, the process for development of the board agendas, when and how you'll check in on a regular basis. As Chair or Lead Director, an important aspect of your role will involve debriefing with the CEO in terms of issues that arise at the board's executive sessions. You might also want to discuss the format for those debriefs – whether they'll be held immediately after the board meeting or the following day.

The board typically doesn't rely on external advisors to the same extent that board committees do, but there's certainly nothing wrong with scheduling some initial conversations with the board's external auditors, compensation consultants, legal counsel, or any other outside resources the board works with on a regular basis.

Meeting Facilitation

The board's work is largely done in its meetings and the facilitation of those meetings is at the very heart of the Chair's role, itself. I've seen numerous instances of directors with far less compelling CVs than their peers named to the role of Board Chair because they're viewed by their colleagues as someone who "knows how to run a good meeting" and who can build a constructive working relationship with the Chief Executive Officer.

All of the points outlined in Chapter Twelve on this subject of meeting facilitation apply equally to a Board Chair in running the board meetings and/or to a Lead Director in facilitating executive sessions. The Chair needs to draw out different perspectives on critical issues, actively listen to the board dialogue and intervene when directors delve into micro-management or go off on tangents. All of this requires the Chair to keep a careful eye on body language in the meeting as well as an eye on the clock. As discussed in Chapter Twelve, the Chair can and should weigh in on the issues, but many consider it advisable to delay doing so until later in the discussion so that their views don't dissuade others from taking a different or contrary position.

At the end of any board discussion, it's critical to provide clear direction to management. A perennial comment from senior executives about their boards is this: "I present to the board, and we have a terrific discussion. All kinds of different ideas are thrown out on the table. Then the Chair says, 'That was great, thank you very much' and I leave. But I have no idea what I'm supposed to do now. Am I supposed to follow up on some of the points that were raised in the meeting? Does it mean, 'Ok, we canvassed this issue and didn't find anything wrong, so you can go ahead'? That's what I typically assume. But I've had situations where a director said to me afterwards, "I thought you were going to look into this or that." Yet, I had no idea that this is something the board expected. A little more clarity in giving direction to management would be really helpful from my perspective."

Two items discussed in Chapter Twelve with respect to committee meetings are even more important when it comes to board meetings: agenda design and pre-reading materials:

- **Board Agendas:** Some agendas are jam-packed; others begin with tedious updates and don't get into critical strategic issues until later in the meeting, when directors are getting tired and the time's getting "crunched". Many agendas seem almost "recycled" from year to year and can often benefit from some refreshment. Consider ways to restructure your meetings slightly to make them more productive. It's also important to establish a vehicle for directors to recommend agenda items, so that the Chair can give these suggestions due consideration and incorporate those that appear worthwhile into upcoming meetings.

- **Board Books:** If this is an area for improvement – as it is at many boards – it's something you should work with the CEO to tackle. Succinct, well-organized materials enable the board to get more readily into the discussion and ask better questions; ponderous board books that don't tell a clear story leave directors going off-topic and getting into detailed questions that might properly be called out as "micro-management". Although board materials are nearly always prepared by management, it's the responsibility of the Board Chair to make sure their board is getting the materials they need for effective board dialogue.

Working Relationship with the CEO

The working relationship between the Chair or Lead Director and the CEO should be a constructive relationship characterized by mutual respect. It shouldn't be marred by evident tensions, nor should it be too cozy. Many Chairs and Lead Directors provide mentorship to new CEOs, giving them guidance about working effectively with the board and insights about the board's history, politics, and dynamics. This guidance can be extremely valuable, as the transition from reporting to one person ("a boss") to a group (the Board of Directors) is a significant challenge for most new Chief Executives.[15]

A Chair or Lead Director needs to be able to deliver tough messages to the CEO on behalf of the board. This is the reason that a "CEO lapdog" or even a preservationist is often a poor choice to serve in this role; neither are reliable bellwethers and often shrink from giving the CEO "bad news". But the opposite approach is problematic as well. A board leader who constantly criticizes management, offers little support or encouragement, and almost never commends "a job well done" will create a cool, if not hostile relationship. Their concerns may be discounted, even when they are valid. Moreover, the CEO will inevitably become quite guarded; rather than creating a tenor of openness, management is more likely to try to cover up any problems, for fear of further criticism and retribution.

There are several ways in which a Board Chair can be particularly helpful to the Chief Executive Officer and ultimately to the board, itself:

    a. **Early warning signal.** The most important way in which a Chair or Lead Director can be of benefit to a Chief Executive Officer is by alerting them to an issue where they are on shaky ground with the board. This enables the CEO to address the situation before it becomes a serious problem. Being able to act in this capacity requires the Chair/Lead Director to maintain a reliable "finger on the pulse" of the board – and that directors remain open in sharing their views. This requires the Board Chair/Lead Director to demonstrate the utmost respect for director confidentiality.

    b. **Sounding board.** A Chair or Lead Director should also be able to serve as a "sounding board" for the CEO on a range of issues. Most CEOs will cite this as the area where their Chair/Lead Director adds the greatest value and makes a real difference. Fulfilling this aspect of the role requires the Chair/Lead Director to have a good understanding of the business, the company, and the industry. It also requires ongoing efforts to keep abreast of developments that have the potential to impact the company – be those economic, regulatory, technological, consumer demographics, changes to the industry landscape, or otherwise.

    c. **Confirm board priorities.** The role of Chief Executive Officer is complex and multi-dimensional. Urgent and important issues arise every day that were never foreseen even a month earlier! It can therefore be important for the Board Chair/Lead Director to reconfirm the board's priorities in their conversations with the CEO to keep management on track in achieving what the board considers the most important objectives for the organization. If something arises that clearly becomes a greater priority than those initially mandated by the board at the start of the year, the Chair/Lead Director needs to clarify this with both the board and the CEO to make sure that management resources are properly directed.

d. **Board communications between meetings.** Typically, the CEO and the Board Chair are in regular communication between the board meetings. An important consideration during these discussions involves the materiality of developments arising between meetings: Which are worthy of notifying directors about immediately? Which can be deferred for an update at the next board meeting? This is an important consideration, as directors need to be well-informed about significant issues impacting the company between meetings. That said, there is seldom much value created by inundating directors with non-essential updates; this can be annoying and may result in micro-management. Sometimes, a CEO will assume that they have "informed the board" of an issue by updating the Chair/Lead Director about the matter, only to later discover the Chair has not passed this on to other board members; they assumed the CEO would do so. Clarity between the Chair and the CEO around these issues can avoid misunderstandings and finger-pointing if an important issue falls between the cracks.

e. **Antidote to Micro-Management.** As discussed earlier, most boards micro-manage in emergency scenarios or where they lose confidence in the CEO and management team. Boards of early stage companies also tend to operate in Hands-On mode, where the board is routinely involved in management-level decisions. In all other circumstances, however, micro-management is inappropriate, frustrating, and distracts the board from its oversight responsibilities. It also alleviates management from the burden of accountability if the board is constantly making management decisions themselves. The best antidote to micro-management is a Board Chair who has a good understanding of the governance/management line and intervenes in board discussions when the line is crossed, reverting board dialogue back to an oversight level. This same type of intervention is required when the board segues from agenda items to unrelated topics and directors' "pet issues".

f. **Gatekeeper on Board Information Requests**: In Chapter Nine, we discussed an ongoing management frustration, namely the numerous follow-up items that emerge from many board meetings. There's a role for the Board Chair to play in this regard as well, which involves serving as somewhat of a gatekeeper to ensure that management isn't inordinately burdened by board requests. If you sense that a director's request for additional or modified information is important – perhaps something management should have included in the pre-reading in the first place, or some added facts that may shed light on an important risk, opportunity, or board decision – there's no need to intervene. But if the information seems unlikely to have much impact, the Chair should ask the CEO how much management time/effort may be required to put the information together. If it's quick and easy, no problem. If not, turn back to the director requesting the information to ask if they think it's worth the effort. If inordinate information requests have been a problem at your board, it can be useful to mention this new practice to the board prior to adopting it. That way, no one will be surprised when you do; they may even self-censor before making some "nice to have" requests in the first place.

Working Relationship with the Board

No board leader can provide an early warning signal to a CEO about potential board concerns or provide useful perspectives about how the board would react to management proposals unless they're in touch with their board members from time to time and understand how they're thinking about the company and its key issues. Some Chairs are scrupulous about this; others only spend time connecting with one or two directors between meetings, typically those with whom they've become close friends.

Many Chairs make a point of meeting with every member of the board once a year; a relatively informal discussion to explore their thoughts on a range of issues. Pre-COVID, they would often fly to the director's hometown to facilitate these discussions, sometimes held over a lunch or dinner. Today, these conversations could readily be accomplished by videoconference. Either way, they tend to be most effective if the Chair or Lead Director structures the conversation just a bit, possibly sending out a few questions in advance as a "discussion starter". Otherwise, they can become little more than a social chat.

It's essential that board leaders respect the confidentiality of directors' comments and confidences – whether those are views expressed in one-on-one meetings or otherwise. Breaching director confidences can not only damage individual relationships, but can also significantly impair the Chair or Lead Director's effectiveness in their role, as directors will become hesitant to share their views.

A debrief with the CEO following a board executive session provides a good example: The Chair or Lead Director needs to outline the key points raised in the executive session without revealing "who said what". This can often be a challenge. CEOs nearly always respond to critical comments by asking, "That was Dan's comment, wasn't it?" When this occurs, the Chair or Lead Director needs to reiterate their obligation to respect the confidentiality of executive sessions. If a board leader violates a director's trust – in a CEO debrief or otherwise – it's not at all easy to rebuild.

One of the most challenging facets of the Board Chair's role involves director performance management. This has become one of the most significant failings of board leadership today. For this reason, Chapter Fourteen has been devoted entirely to this subject. It outlines several director performance management tools that every Chair or Lead Director should know about.

Ambassadorial Role/Special Assignments

Some CEOs ask their Chair or Lead Director to accompany them to meetings with major shareholders; the CEO speaks for the company, but on certain issues it may be worthwhile for an independent board leader to join those conversations. Executive Chairs of family-controlled companies who are descendants of the founder(s) are often viewed as "corporate royalty" and nearly always play a significant ambassadorial role with employees, in the community, and often with suppliers, customers, and other stakeholders. And needless to say, if a crisis grips the company that results in the CEO being terminated or otherwise sidelined, the Chair or Lead Director needs to play a role at the forefront of the situation in dealing with the media and other key stakeholders.

Many Chairs and Lead Directors also take on special assignments, such as leading a special board committee. Typically, the Chair plays an important role in CEO succession planning, even if these efforts are formally led by the HR/Compensation Committee or an ad hoc CEO Succession Committee chaired by another director. Any incoming CEO will place a premium on their impressions of the Chair/Lead Director when making a decision about the CEO role: Is this someone they believe they can build a constructive working relationship with? Do they have a background that would make them an excellent "sounding board" on critical corporate issues and a good mentor, early in the CEO's tenure? Do they think they'd genuinely enjoy working with this Chair or Lead Director?

Most Board Chairs also play an important role in director recruitment, even though these efforts are led by the Nominating and Governance Committee. No director worth their salt would join a board without meeting the Chair or Lead Director and forming a positive impression in this regard. I've even had directors tell me, "The main reason I joined this board was because of [name of Chair]. He is such an impressive guy – and I knew I'd not only enjoy working with him, I'd learn a lot, as a director. I also knew he'd undoubtedly lead an outstanding board. I wanted to be a part of that!"

Tone at the Top

Every director serves as a role model – to executives, employees, and even their fellow board members – but none has greater impact than the Board Chair. A truly great chair is the embodiment of the company's values. In fact, one of the best Chairs I've ever worked with got exactly this feedback in her last evaluation from board members and top executives, one of the highest compliments any Chair can receive.

Great Board Chairs and Lead Directors work hard to earn the admiration of their peers and the organization they govern, which often requires them to make tough and sometimes unpopular decisions. The board, after all, is the place where "the buck is supposed to stop" in any company – and it is the Chair more than anyone else on the board who needs to hold management accountable for the company's performance and reputation.

They must also scrupulously avoid decisions and practices that can detract from their credibility. In many cases, this is not so much what they do, but what they ignore – turning a blind eye to shoddy management performance or questionable CEO decisions, continuing to use a compensation consultant who recommends CEO pay levels that are difficult to justify and, perhaps the most common problem of all, ignoring director performance issues that are evident to members of the board and the executive team.

Chapter Fourteen

DIRECTOR PERFORMANCE MANAGEMENT

DIRECTOR PERFORMANCE MANAGEMENT is one of the biggest shortcomings in corporate governance today. In Chapter One, I referenced PriceWaterhouse Coopers' 2020 Annual Directors study of almost 700 US public company directors, wherein 49% expressed the view that at least one of their fellow directors should be replaced and 21% thought that two or more should go.[16] Directors in the PwC study gave board leadership their lowest marks in the area director performance management; one in four (25%) rated their board leaders as either "not very" or "not at all" effective in dealing with director performance problems.[17]

Board Chairs need to step up to director performance issues rather than shy away from them; their credibility will be compromised if they don't. Other directors and senior corporate executives know who's carrying their weight in the boardroom – and who is not.

It's tough to tell a boardroom colleague who's had a stellar business career that they have to "shape up or ship out" if they're clearly not performing. Many Chairs would rather avoid these awkward conversations. Instead, they rely on age and term limits to stimulate board turnover. When the director hits the mandatory retirement age, they're off the board – no questions asked.

However, age and term limits are ineffective as director performance management tools. Most director performance problems have nothing to do with the director's age or the length of time they've served on the board. A director who routinely arrives unprepared for meetings, eats up half the meeting time with off-topic remarks, and uses a patronizing tone with colleagues could just as easily be conducting themselves this way at 52 as 72. And if they *are* 52, they could theoretically be re-nominated for a very long time unless a boardroom champion steps up to address the problem.

There are four director performance management tools every board leader should know about:

- Director Expectations
- Director Evaluations
- Board 2.0 (the best board succession planning tool I've ever found); and
- New Director 360s.

This chapter provides an overview of the first three; New Director 360s have already been discussed in Chapter Seven. If you're looking for more in-depth information on Director Evaluations and Board

2.0, beyond the overviews in this chapter, you might consider picking up a copy of *Board and Director Evaluations: Innovations for 21st Century Governance Committees.*[18]

Director Expectations

Director Expectations (Appendix C-1) serve to establish and reinforce what's expected of board members. It's the easiest performance management tool to implement, but it has relatively low impact. Some companies create a parallel document that outlines Expectations of Management in Working with the Board (Appendix C-2).

The quick and easy way to approach Director Expectations is to simply recraft Appendices C-1 and C-2, send a draft around the board for comment, make a few modifications, and call it a day. But this approach has almost no impact. Director Expectations only pack a punch when they involve interviews with every member of the board at the outset to gather their views: What do they expect of their boardroom peers? What do they expect of management in working with the board? What can and should management be able to expect from board members?

The Expectations you'll create from these conversations will probably look a lot like Appendices C-1 and C-2. But there's a crucial difference: Directors have now become engaged and given these questions some thought; this serves to reinforce their importance and cultivate buy-in. Don't be at all surprised if you notice some positive changes after the Expectations are developed and discussed by the board: Some directors will start to prepare more diligently for meetings. Others will make a point of listening more and showing greater respect for contrary positions. Still others may increase their efforts to keep abreast of industry developments.

While nice to see, these changes are frequently short-lived. However, once developed, director expectations can be used both in director recruitment and director performance management, a useful component of your director performance management toolkit.

Director Evaluations

Over the past 25 years, I've conducted dozens of director evaluations. The process I currently use is summarized in Appendix D. Three elements have proven to be particularly important in designing a director evaluation process that's genuinely worthwhile:

- First, I've found it optimal to collect director evaluation feedback through interviews, which facilitate probing questions to draw out specific examples and clarify key points. Numerical scores have several drawbacks – low scores anger recipients without providing useful insights about what's wrong; high scores fail to reinforce a director's strengths. Some write-in comments are vague; others are downright nasty. Although some boards believe a "low score" can indicate whether a director should be re-nominated, a far better approach, in my view, is to eliminate the scoring and simply ask the question outright: "Should Director X be re-nominated for another term?"

- Second, having the feedback collected by an external facilitator ensures confidentiality and prevents directors from dismissing negative comments by attributing these to a "personality conflict" with the Chair or other internal interviewer. An externally facilitated process is also viewed as far more credible by company executives.

- Third, the feedback board members receive should be constructive, actionable, and balanced; this is what makes the evaluation process truly worthwhile from the recipient's perspective. Directors need to clearly understand their strengths, contributions, and areas for improvement. Actionable feedback enables them to know how to address any shortcomings that emerge. It's equally important that the feedback is balanced. Every board member – even underperformers – should receive both positive comments that reinforce their strengths and suggestions on where they could be more effective. Perhaps ironically, it's often the best board members who most value suggestions for improvement, so it's important to probe for these kernels of useful advice. "Problem directors" on the other hand, are far more likely to accept negative feedback when they also receive some genuine appreciation for what they've done well.

Director evaluations are far more than a trap for underperforming board members. When properly designed, director evaluations can help *all* board members better understand their strengths and enhance their effectiveness as directors.

Few of us genuinely like getting feedback. But there's nothing more important for professional development. An effective director evaluation not only takes aim at performance problems, it reinforces the contributions of your boardroom stars, which can be every bit as important in building your board into a high-performing governance team.

Director evaluations designed along these lines are the best tool I've ever found to address director performance issues that are behavioral in nature. Some director "problems" are actually a pretty quick fix once the board member gets the kind of feedback just described:

The director either stops doing something that's detracting from their performance (such as taking the board down rabbit holes at every meeting), starts doing something differently (such as better preparation for meetings) or modifies their boardroom conduct (such as rolling their eyes when another director expresses a view they disagree with).

In my experience, roughly 80% of directors who get constructive and actionable suggestions for improvement, try to take appropriate action once they understand the problem.

But what if the root of the issue is not a behavioral problem, but stems instead from the director's expertise? A good example of this is the former CEO of a coal company who serves as a director of "ABC Energy". Let's call him Curtis. Curtis was a great contributor when ABC was involved in mining. But ABC sold its coal mines three years ago and invested in wind turbines. Now, Curtis has very little to say. A director evaluation will let Curtis know that he's no longer seen as a strong boardroom contributor. But, in practical terms, there's not a lot Curtis can do to remedy the problem. Sure, he can read up on wind farms and go to an industry conference – but that's never going to allow Curtis to make the type of contributions the ABC board would get if they replaced Curtis with another director who'd spent years in the wind industry.

This is a far more insidious problem than a behavioral issue. As one Fortune 500 Board Chair noted, "You can teach people about governance; there are plenty of courses for that. But you can't change what they've spent 20 or 30 years doing in their executive careers." And if this lies at the heart of a director performance issue on your board – if it's the real reason many of your directors think a boardroom colleague should be replaced – a director evaluation is *not* the best tool to address it. You'd do much better with a board succession planning tool, such as Board 2.0.

Board 2.0

Board 2.0 is the best board succession planning tool I've ever found. It engages every member of the board in designing the optimal board composition to govern the company in 3–5 years' time.

This section provides a very quick overview of Board 2.0. You may well have other questions about using Board 2.0, including board size, how to factor diversity (gender, race, age, geography) and personal characteristics (integrity, leadership, commitment) into optimizing your board composition, all of which are essential considerations.[19] But for the purposes of this overview, I'm going to focus on how to use Board 2.0 as a performance management tool in a situation similar to ABC Energy – a director whose background/expertise is no longer germane to the business.

Here's how Board 2.0 works: Using a template along the lines of Figure 14.1, draw the number of circles around the "board table" equal to the size of your board. Each circle represents a seat at the board table. One seat is typically allocated to the CEO.

Each board member participating in the Board 2.0 exercise is asked to consider the skills, experience and/or background of the person they'd want to have in each remaining seat at the future board table, so as to create the best possible mix of expertise to oversee the company in 3–5 years' time.

Long-term corporate strategy needs to be considered. For example, in 3–5 years' time a US hospitality company may anticipate having several properties in Mexico and the Caribbean; a biotech currently focused on scientific research may have succeeded in taking a drug to market. Would these changes impact your views on the expertise necessary to have at the board table to create the best possible governance team to oversee your company in three years' time?

Figure 14.1: Board 2.0

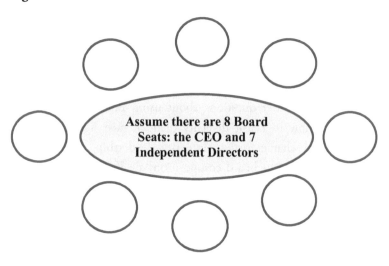

Don't worry about the backgrounds of the directors currently serving on your board and don't put any names in the circles; they should *only* reflect expertise. As you "allocate" your board seats, try to be specific. For example, avoid simply allocating one or two seats for "financial expertise"; be clear as to whether you believe the best director would be someone with a Chief Financial Officer background, a Big Four Audit Partner, an investment banker, a commercial banker, or a different finance background altogether. All would offer financial expertise, but each would bring a very different perspective to the board discussions.

Avoid using Board 2.0 as a group exercise. For example, if Curtis were sitting in the room, how comfortable would ABC board members be in saying, "I don't think we need coal expertise on the ABC board going forward"? Board 2.0 will only be effective with confidential, individual one-on-ones that are then analyzed and compiled to create a "working draft" of Board 2.0 for further discussion.

Each Board 2.0 chart that results from an individual interview represents the participant's views on the optimal composition of the future board. When interviews with every member of the board have been completed, no two charts may be exactly the same. But in every Board 2.0 exercise that I've been involved with, there has always been significant agreement among directors about the majority of the board seats – for example, for a board of eight directors, you'll likely find substantial agreement about five or six of the seats and terrific suggestions on the rest. Because every director is given an opportunity to weigh in on this important question, board alignment on the final Board 2.0 design is often reached quite easily after the draft is considered and discussed with the entire board.

So, what happens to Curtis – or to any sitting board member whose background/expertise isn't included in Board 2.0? After all, it's unlikely that the final Board 2.0 chart for ABC Energy is going to include "coal mining expertise". While this outcome may provide some momentary drama, it's almost inevitable, given that Board 2.0 is the "next generation" of the board's composition. It will undoubtedly differ somewhat from the board you have today.

When this occurs, it's important to remember two things: (i) Board 2.0 is the optimal composition for the board in 3–5 years' time, not next week; and (ii) the pacing of any board transitions to achieve Board 2.0 remains entirely at the discretion of the Nominating and Governance Committee. Practically speaking, it is nearly always the director's contributions and effectiveness that weigh most heavily into the Committee's decisions.

This is what typically happens: The Nominating and Governance Committee sets about recruiting one or two directors to fill in the gaps necessary to create Board 2.0. The board agrees to temporarily expand in size, to facilitate a smooth transition to Board 2.0, which includes "planned overlap" between incoming and outgoing directors. To use the ABC example, Curtis stays on the board while this occurs.

Within twelve months, this recruitment is typically accomplished. Board 2.0 is seldom fully developed at this stage, but one or two evident gaps in board expertise necessary to create Board 2.0 have been filled. For Curtis, the "writing's on the wall". Directors in this situation frequently resign or offer not to stand for re-election when their term expires. But it's up to the Nominating and Governance Committee whether to accept their resignation.

If they don't offer to resign and the Committee feels it's time for them to go, the Committee chair may simply tell this director that they're not being re-nominated. These are never easy conversations, but they're much more straightforward once a Board 2.0 exercise has pre-paved the whole matter: "As you know, Curtis, we need to make this change sooner or later. Now that we've recruited two new board members …"

But here's a critical point: Board 2.0 creates a lever for the Committee. When that lever is pulled is *entirely* at the Committee's discretion. In practical terms, it's nearly always determined by a director's contributions and performance. The situation with Curtis could go one of two ways:

    i. If Curtis has barely said a word since the coal mines were sold, the Committee is likely to either accept Curtis's resignation or have a "tough conversation" with Curtis the next time he's up for re-nomination;

ii. Maybe Curtis isn't saying much in the board meetings, and everyone agrees that coal expertise is no longer necessary on the ABC board, *but* Curtis is the Chair of the Compensation Committee and he's terrific in this role. He held the line on bonuses last year despite hours of CEO grumbling and earned the CEO's genuine respect. Nobody wants Curtis to leave. That's fine! Curtis stays. The Nominating and Governance Committee can continue to re-nominate him, despite the Board 2.0 result. Who cares if the board expands by one seat during the transition and even a bit beyond if this allows one of the board's most valuable directors to remain at the table?

Board 2.0 is a tool not a rule – one that works particularly well when the director performance "problem" largely relates to a director's expertise and background.

Chair Evaluations

Any Board Chair or Lead Director willing to step up to director performance management issues needs to lead by example. This means adopting a Chair evaluation process, as well.

I don't believe it's necessary to undertake a Chair evaluation annually; every three years seems to work well. But it *is* essential to design a process that's both credible and genuinely useful in terms of providing worthwhile feedback. Self-evaluations are something to avoid; they lack credibility and attract management derision: "Can I conduct my own performance appraisal this year, just like our Chair does?"

In Britain, the *UK Corporate Governance Code* recommends that FTSE 350 companies appoint both a Non-Executive Chair and a Senior Independent Director. The remit of the latter is to conduct a regular appraisal of the Chair's performance with the full board. The Code also recommends that FTSE 350s use an external facilitator for their board evaluations every three years.[20]

Within the S&P1500, where boards typically appoint either a Non-Executive Chair or Lead Director as leader of the independent directors, the British concept has never caught on. However, some US boards ask the Chair of the Nominating and Governance Committee to lead an evaluation of the Board Chair, which is essentially the same process. If they were to add an externally facilitated evaluation every three years, they'd actually be operating in parallel with the UK recommendations.

The director evaluation process outlined earlier works just as well for Chair evaluations as for any other director, the only difference being that the protocol for a Chair evaluation should be deliberately expanded to cover all key facets of the Chair role discussed in Chapter Thirteen.

There are two important reasons that boardroom champions develop and adopt a robust Chair evaluation process:

    i. First, it demonstrates a commitment to continuous improvement, not only for the board, but for its leader. Receiving meaningful, constructive feedback, as described in the section on director evaluations, can provide worthwhile insights to any Board Chair, enabling them to understand where they're perceived as making particularly strong contributions and where there may yet be opportunities to be even better in leading the board. Preservationists, on the other hand, are terrified of feedback, fearing that it may highlight some of their shortcomings and threaten their continued tenure. Interestingly, in many instances true boardroom champions almost brush off their numerous well-deserved accolades: "That's all very nice," they've told me in discussing their feedback, "But what I really want to understand is what I can do better."

ii. Second, boardroom champions understand the importance of setting the right tone at the top. The Board Chair is in a unique position to set that cultural tone, not only for the board but for the entire company and to reinforce corporate values. A robust Chair evaluation reflects a commitment to excellence and accountability at the very apex of the organization.

PART V
Parting Thoughts

Chapter Fifteen

PROVE THEM RIGHT

AS I WAS finishing the manuscript for this book, I got two phone calls that were particularly timely. The first was from a retired Chief Human Resources Officer of a Fortune 500 company, who I'll call Jennifer. Jennifer had wanted to serve on a public company board for years and had reached out tirelessly to people in her business network to try to make that happen. She told me that she'd just been invited to join the board of a very interesting midcap company. I expected her to be excited. But Jennifer was cynical: "I know they only asked me to join the board so that they could say they had another woman at the board table."

"Do you still like the idea of serving on a board?" I asked her. "Of course! I've wanted to be on a board for years; you know that." "Do you like this company? Do you like the CEO? Do you think you'll enjoy the issues that you'll be dealing with as a director?" "Oh, yes!" she told me, "I think this company has a great future and the CEO is amazing." "Then prove them right," I told her, "This board invited you to be a director. You want to be a director – and you want to be on the board of this company; you just told me that. You're a little skeptical about some directors' motives in selecting you, but my best advice is this: Prove them right. Prove to them that inviting you to serve on this board was one of the best damn decisions they ever made!"

The following day, I got a call from someone I'll call Henry, a long-serving director on a board that doesn't have a retirement age. Henry, himself, had fought diligently against it, arguing that an "arbitrary retirement age" discounted a director's contributions and merits. "Well, they just re-nominated me," Henry chuckled, "I think they felt that they had to!" "Do you want to stay on the board?" I asked him, "After all, you've served for fifteen years. Is it still fun? Is it still rewarding?" Henry paused for a moment, "Yes, it is. I'm thrilled at how we've built this company; I want to continue to be on the board. The fact that I know our history and what we've been through is very helpful in board discussions. However, I think there are some directors who feel I'm getting a bit long in the tooth."

"But they re-nominated you, right?" "I think some felt they had no choice," Henry replied. "Well, I think you need to prove them right," I told him. "Prove to your board that they made the right decision re-nominating you. Prove that you're still a terrific director who makes solid contributions and serves as a great role model for other board members and for the executive team."

This is the advice I'd give to any director on the board of any organization at any point in their board career. And it's the advice that I'd offer you as a parting thought: If a Board of Directors has chosen to nominate or re-nominate you, prove that it was a good decision – no, a great decision – to have you at the board table. I hope that this book will be helpful to you in accomplishing this worthwhile objective, and I wish you all the best in a truly noble undertaking: that of becoming a boardroom star.

APPENDICES

Appendix A:

PREREQUISITES TO COLLABORATIVE/ OVERSIGHT

Many boards today are seeking to evolve their operating mode from the traditional Reporting Out approach to the Collaborative/Oversight model. But even Boards that are inspired to make this shift, often can't accomplish it quickly. That's because there are a number of requirements necessary. One or more of these will be gaps in the way the board is operating right now – even if the board itself is already high-functioning. These are the four essential prerequisites necessary to successfully adopt a Collaborative/Oversight model:

- **Board materials and presentations**: The Collaborative/Oversight model requires a shift in the way management works with the board – fostering board engagement rather than management simply "telling their story" in board meetings and then "fending off" directors' questions. The cadence of the Collaborative/Oversight relationship is synergistic, rather than "Here's what we want to do" followed by "Okay, any questions?" This necessitates a different tone in the way board presentations are framed and in the design of the board materials provided prior to the meetings. Board materials are an area where many management teams could improve. Some executives throw "everything but the kitchen sink" into their board books and repurpose materials from executive presentations in order to save time. But a board audience is quite different than a team of industry executives who spend every day focused on the company's business. And far too often, detailed materials and re-purposed presentations unwittingly lead the board in the opposite direction: towards Micro-Management. If your ultimate goal is to transition your board to the Collaborative/Oversight model, even well-comprised board books and terrific presentations will nonetheless require some refinement to achieve this.

- **Board Chair facilitation skills:** An effective Collaborative/Oversight discussion requires an excellent meeting facilitator to draw people into the dialogue, shut down off-topic segues, actively listen, keep the board focused and the conversation energized, strive for a balance in terms of guidance and challenges from the board, drive to a consensus decision and summarize that decision to provide clarity to management. Now, one might argue that this is what an effective Chair needs to do in running *any* board meeting. But the truth is, not all Chairs have these skills. And it's a lot easier to chair a Reporting Out style of meeting where the role can be fulfilled by acting as little more than a traffic director – "First Mark, then Sheryl."

- **Board composition:** The Collaborative/Oversight model works best when board members have a good understanding of the company's business and relevant experience that enables them to serve as a collaborative thought partner to the CEO and management team. The model presumes there is high intellect at your board table, which is nearly always the case. But it also necessitates relevant expertise that would be genuinely worthwhile to bring into play more vibrantly on critical corporate issues. If that's not the case, discussions generated from the Collaborative/Oversight approach will inevitably disappoint. Only if you have the right people at the board table is it worth the effort to make the shift to the Collaborative/Oversight model. Many boards find that they need to recruit at least two new directors with expertise not currently resident at the board table to bolster their existing board talent if they're serious about creating the board composition necessary to make the Collaborative/Oversight shift really worthwhile; some need even more.

- **CEO sets appropriate parameters:** Some CEOs are concerned about the Collaborative/ Oversight model because they fear it threatens their control and decision-making by allowing the board to become far more engaged. It's true that board engagement will increase, and the dynamics of the board/management relationship will also change with this shift. But savvy CEOs realize that there's a Goldilocks formula that can facilitate the shift, without creating headaches. It all comes down to their ability – as CEO – to set appropriate parameters in working with the board.

Let's use this simple example as an illustration: The company's Chief Financial Officer is retiring at the end of the year. Some CEOs will simply tell the board, "I've just hired Jane Smith as my new CFO." Executive staffing decisions, after all, are entirely within the CEO's purview and the CEO exercised complete control over that decision – and that's what many would do with a board operating in Reporting Out mode.

At the other extreme, a CEO trying to have a "more open board relationship" might say: "Here are three CVs from our headhunter for a new CFO. I want your input – which one of these strikes you as the best candidate?" But this goes too far in the other direction; the CEO just ceded the CFO decision to the board – and if they don't like the board's opinion, they're into a testy argument.

A savvy CEO striving for a Collaborative/Oversight relationship might take an approach along these lines: "We are about to conduct a search for a new CFO. I'm inclined to restrict that search to people with experience in our industry. Does anyone disagree – and if you'd broaden the search, why would you do so? I've asked the Chair of the Audit Committee to interview the final CFO candidate before I offer the job to him or her. What I'd love to get from every other director – and you can email me – is one question you'd encourage me to ask CFO candidates once we get to the interview stage." The CEO remains entirely in control of the CFO decision but collaborates with the board on important aspects of the process. Not every CEO knows how to set these kinds of parameters.

Appendix B

SAMPLE NEW DIRECTOR 360: INDIVIDUAL DIRECTOR FEEDBACK REPORT

Prepared for: Deborah Richards

Overview

This individual director feedback report has been compiled to reflect themes and sample comments (*in italics*) from the New Director 360 for Deborah Richards. This process involved a series of interviews with all members of the ABC Board of Directors, four members of the ABC executive team and a representative of Ernst & Young, ABC's external auditor. The interviews were conducted by Skype between January 26 and February 8, 2019.

Interviewees were asked to provide their views on Deborah's strengths and contributions as a new director of ABC based on their experience working with her over the past 12 months since she joined the board. They were also asked to offer advice or identify any areas for improvement that could further enhance Deborah's effectiveness and contributions to the ABC Board going forward. Over 100 individual comments were generated from the interviews. These have been summarized, analyzed, and grouped into key themes presented in this report.

Major Strengths/Contributions

Deborah's major strength, as the sitting Chief Financial Officer of a large global company, is clearly her wealth of expertise on a broad range of financial issues. She has already added tremendous value to Audit Committee discussions and in her meetings with Internal Audit, where she served as a sounding board for the IA team on a broad range of issues. Most of Deborah's board colleagues cited her contributions to the board's discussions about changing ABC's dividend policy as one of her most significant contributions to date; Deborah drew on her experience to challenge ABC's longstanding views around this issue – and changed the board's thinking.

- *"We are extremely fortunate to have someone with Deborah's vast array of financial expertise at our board table. And the fact that she is a sitting CFO is really the 'icing on the cake' because she is so current on the issues and brings such relevant and insightful perspectives. I particularly commend her for making the time to sit down with Internal Audit not only at her orientation session – which lasted two hours longer than it was supposed to – but also at another meeting a few months later. She spent time getting to know the people in IA and created* a nice, informal environment where everyone was comfortable just kicking around some of the issues and getting the benefit of her wisdom and experience. It was invaluable."

- "Deborah has rejuvenated our Audit Committee. Everyone in those meetings – particularly our own IA team and even E&Y – are benefiting from her contributions. She backs them up, at times, and you can tell they appreciate that because she comes at these issues from a very solid knowledge base. She is also respectful of our Audit Chair – and I feel that's important to mention as well. Deborah is clearly very conscious not to overstep and essentially 'take over the committee', which she could easily do. That shows a lot of maturity and professionalism; it's something I've really admired about her."

- "The reason we recruited Deborah to the board was for her financial expertise – and she has already gone above and beyond in this domain. Her comments and questions, particularly in the Audit Committee, reflect her depth of knowledge and currency; she brings and draws on a wealth of experience and challenges the way we've viewed things in the past. Perhaps the most evident example of this relates to the board debate around the dividend, where she encouraged the board to consider some different perspectives – and, as a result, we changed our policy. I also think it was Deborah's approach that made all the difference – clearly, she had wrestled with this issue personally, as a CFO, and could bring all of that to bear. But she offered her views in a generous way, by which I mean she didn't feel the need to make the people who held a different view 'wrong' so that she could be 'right'."

- "When Deborah speaks – particularly on financial issues – people listen. In her first or second board meeting, an issue

> about our dividend came up and Deborah made some great points about the changing dynamics of our shareholder base. This was the kind of issue where a new director could actually get out on a limb and lose credibility, as she was challenging some longstanding views. But she triumphed! That was the moment that Deborah kind of 'earned her wings' with this board, and she hasn't looked back."

- > "The dividend has been a sacred cow at this company for as long as I can remember. And Deborah literally took that bull by the horns – and changed the board's thinking. That, in my view, is her most significant contribution to date, but it's the most significant of many. Deborah is well on her way to becoming one of ABC's best directors, in my opinion."

Deborah's contributions to discussions on M&A integration have also been particularly insightful – and notable because the most important of these related to corporate culture, rather than finance. This demonstrated Deborah's breadth as a director and prompted the board to engage in a critical debate that added significant value for the management team, leveraging, among other things, her own learnings from another M&A integration experience.

- > "One of the things our management team has really struggled with is M&A integration. Everybody wants to do the deal – but the integration piece hasn't always gone smoothly. This is an area where Deborah can and already has made major contributions – and interestingly, this was not related to finance. She spoke up about the cultural integration issues of the XYZ deal and explained, in very practical terms, how this became a huge obstacle in a deal she had worked on a few years back, which also involved the acquisition of a founder-controlled company. Everybody on the board was absolutely riveted when she described this, and she brought up points that I don't think anyone else on the board – or in management – had even considered."

- "Deborah has had a long track record of doing M&A deals as a CFO and even before that. She understands deal structure, and she is particularly well-attuned to the issues involved in successful MA& integration – which is something we've struggled with in the past. Having the benefit of her insights in these discussions is incredibly valuable not only to the board, but also to the management team."

- "One thing that perhaps surprised me – because I tend to think of Deborah as a finance expert – is that she really gets 'people issues' too. This came to the fore in our discussions around the XYZ acquisition. She made some great points on financial issues involved in the deal – and I kind of expected that. But then she weighed in on the 'people issues' involved in integrating a founder-led company into a large public company, recounting her experience when 1-2-3 acquired 4-5-6. She described what she learned from this – and what 1-2-3 should have done differently. This opened up a terrific board discussion, and I think management walked out of that meeting saying, "Wow! That's what a good board does for a management team!" And we wouldn't have had that discussion had Deborah not raised the points that she did."

- "Probably most people will say that Deborah's most significant contribution to the board to date involved the dividend issue. But I actually think it was the conversation she initiated around the integration of the XYZ deal. We tend to look at the deal financing and the projected synergies – but Deborah really got us to look 'under the covers' at some of the practical issues of trying to merge a proud, successful founder-led company into a F500 and that was one of the best board discussions I think we've had this year."

Deborah clearly does her homework for board meetings and is extremely well-prepared. It's evident that she has not just read the materials but has given considerable thought to the issues at hand. She 'picks her spots' and tends to weigh in only where she has a different perspective or new angle on the topic, rather than simply reinforcing and building upon the comments of others.

- "It's very apparent from the questions Deborah raises and the comments she makes in board meetings that she's not only read the board briefing materials, she's actually reflected on the issues and has taken some pains to try to think of an angle that we may not have considered. She also picks her spots; she doesn't weigh in on everything – when she dives into the board discussion, you know she's going to raise a new perspective that nobody else has mentioned – or probably even thought of. Every so often, the point she makes is a bit 'off the wall' – but that's fine; that's refreshing sometimes, and it doesn't happen much. Eight times out of ten, she's spot on and is making a big difference in terms of our discussion."

- "One of my biggest concerns when we were recruiting Deborah was whether she'd really have the time to be on our board; after all, she's a sitting CFO at a large, global company. But any fears I may have had on that front have been long dispelled. Not only does she come well prepared, it's evident that she's really thought about the issues and has made some decisions about where she's going to weigh in, so as to try to add real value. That, in my view, is what a really top-notch director does, and she's already got it down cold."

- *"There are two things that really drive me nuts in board meetings – and maybe they drive Deborah nuts too, as a CFO at her own company, because she is studiously avoiding both: The first is people who have clearly not read the board package – they waste everybody's time asking questions that were already covered in the briefings. Deborah would never dream of doing that; it's evident that she's read it all, and she's made notes. The second is people who take up a lot of board time agreeing with what someone else has said – rather than offering a different view. Sometimes I think these people just want to say something to get their name in the minutes. Well, that is certainly not Deborah's style and that is very much to her credit. When Deborah speaks up, she is nearly always injecting a fresh perspective or raising a point that no one else has mentioned. I think that's one of her most important strengths as a board member."*

Deborah's colleagues describe her as "warm, friendly, and approachable"; they genuinely enjoy working with her. She's viewed as professional, respectful of others, a good team player, and a terrific role model for female executives.

- *"Deborah is a very warm person who's enjoyable to be with – and to work with. You get the sense that Deborah genuinely wants to contribute to the board as a team player, she's not someone who has to be a star. Now, in fairness, she's becoming a star and I think that's great – but she doesn't seem have a lot of ego in the room. She's respectful of everyone."*

- *"I think one of Deborah's strengths is that she's a good team player. She doesn't try to dominate the board discussion and you don't get the sense she's going to walk out the door in a huff if the board doesn't agree with her point of view; she's mature and professional."*

- *"The more I get to know Deborah, the better I like her. She's funny, warm, and inclusive – she brings people into conversations and makes a real effort to be part of the team. We could not have made a better choice than recruiting Deborah to become a member of our board, and we're extremely fortunate to have her."*

- *"I expected to be kind of intimidated by Deborah because hey – she's Deborah Richards, the CFO of 1-2-3 Corp. Well, I could not have been more pleasantly surprised! She's approachable and friendly – a really warm person who is very enjoyable to be with. She demonstrates respect for everyone – even the catering lady that comes into the board meetings. There is no better role model for our female executives than Deborah."*

Advice/Potential Areas for Improvement

The more that Deborah continues to learn about ABC's business and the unique facets of its industry, the more she can contribute. This is the area where her colleagues would encourage her to focus and made a number of constructive suggestions for her consideration, including site visits, discussions with operating executives below the C-suite, learning more about ABC's regulatory environment, attending an industry conference and/or reading trade journals. As a sitting CFO, Deborah is extremely time-constrained – something her board colleagues recognize. They nonetheless believe that, if she can manage it, some further investment in her learning will yield tremendous benefits to Deborah personally, and to the ABC board.

- *"Deborah is very time-constrained because she is a sitting CFO – and I recognize that. But she has the potential to become one of our best directors. Making that step to what I'll call 'the next* level' in her board development will require Deborah to invest more time in learning about the operational side of ABC's business. She's a quick study, and I don't think it will take that long. But she has no background in this industry and frankly, it shows in some of her comments. The more she understands the business context and the industry fundamentals, the greater her contributions will be. I'd encourage her – in the very strongest terms – to try to make some time for this. I believe it will yield significant benefits to her personally, as well as to the board, in terms of her contributions."

- "I hate to even say this because Deborah has so much on her plate – but if I were going to give her any advice, it would be to invest the time it takes to learn more about the operational side of ABC's business. I don't think she's been to any of the plants, yet. And I know personally that just one or two site visits can give you a very different perspective – one site visit is worth a hundred PowerPoint slides! So, if I were her, I'd make that a priority. We run our operations 24/7 and if it's easier for her to go on a weekend, that's fine. We have a corporate jet – we'll pick her up and fly her there. We realize she's busy, and we need to make this easy for her. But it's something that we should try to arrange in the next few months."

- "I think the obvious advice to Deborah at this stage is to continue to learn about ABC's business. She's got the finance part down cold. And, as a director, she could just stay in that mode as one of the board's "finance experts" and still add a lot of value. But from what I've seen – especially some of her comments on M&A integration – Deborah has the potential to engage more broadly on strategic issues and really become someone who can guide this company's future. If she wants to make that leap – which I'd personally encourage her to do – then she needs to get a solid feel for this business and the critical factors in this industry: Who are the players and what are the global trends? What are the implications of our regulatory environment in practical terms? One 'quick and dirty' way to get up to speed is to go to the annual conference in Las Vegas – even for one day; that's a 'master class.' But if she can't find the time for that, then make an effort to read the trade journals, get out to the sites and try to spend time (even on a video conference) with some of the operating folks at the regional level."

- "Orientation is a 'drinking from a firehose' experience for most directors – and I'm sure it was for Deborah. Her orientation was focused on finance – meetings with E&Y, the finance team, etc. The operational part of the business was kind of a 'flyover' – and that's where I'd encourage her to focus now. She has no background in this industry, and there's a lot to learn. She's extremely smart and has picked up a lot already – but I'd encourage her to work with the GC to plan out an Orientation Part Two now that she's been on the board for a year. It shouldn't be a one-day thing – it should extend over the course of the year and respect her limited time. It could involve a couple of site visits, one now and another six months from now – an old plant and one of the new ones. I'd have her meet with some of the operations people and some of the regulatory people; she has never worked in an industry with this level of regulation. I know this will require a concerted effort on her part, but I'd look at it as an investment that will pay back huge dividends over the coming years."

- "When we recruited Deborah, she told us that she wanted the experience of serving on an outside board so that she could be a better CFO at her own company – and as professional development if she ever became a CEO. Having seen her in the boardroom, there is no doubt in my mind that a CEO role lies somewhere in her future. I think she can help herself achieve her development goals if she invests the time to learn more about ABC's business – so that she can become a true strategic partner of our CEO and our board rather than just 'a finance specialist'."

- "Deborah has earned a lot of fans on the board in the short time she's been with us. But what's getting in her way is the fact that she doesn't understand certain facets of the business – and every so often she'll make a comment that underscores this and detracts from her credibility. She needs to make an effort to continue to learn about the operational side of the business. You're not going to become an expert overnight – no one expects that! But if she organizes a few meetings with our top operational people as a sort of second phase of orientation, I think that would cover a lot of ground. She should also get out to the plants."

- "I think the obvious advice to Deborah is to continue her learning journey about ABC's business. But one piece of advice I'd mention in conjunction with that is: part of what's been really terrific about Deborah's contributions to date is that she's challenged our thinking about how ABC does things. I believe that the reason Deborah can offer fresh perspectives has something to do with the fact that she comes from a different industry. I don't want her to lose that! But learning about ABC's business shouldn't mean that she can't continue to challenge its norms."

At times, Deborah has allowed herself to become distracted by her electronic devices in meetings. While this temptation can be difficult to avoid – particularly for a sitting CFO – she would do well to become more cognizant of this issue and try to curtail it somewhat.

- "Deborah is a terrific director and I have no advice to give her other than to be a bit more mindful about what I'll call electronic distractions. She's constantly reading and returning emails during the Audit Committee meeting – maybe less at the board meeting, but I've seen it there too. I don't really think it's a case of not paying attention – all her questions are right on point. It's more the optics of this to the people presenting to the Committee."

- "Deborah is awesome! She is a fantastic addition to our board. She is so good that the one thing that drives me nuts is the fact that we never seem to have her full attention. She's fully present in the meeting one minute – and then she's focused on her iPhone. And really focused – like you can see in her face that something is going on that is not good and seems urgent. And that distracts you too. You start to wonder, 'Hmm … I wonder what's happening over at Deborah's company; must be some problem.' Then you realize that you need to revert your own attention back to the Audit Committee. Is it a huge problem? No. Is it something she should try to curtail a bit? Probably, yes."

- "I serve on another board where we all have to place our phones into a box before we go into the board meeting. I don't want to implement this sort of policy at ABC; people need their phones, they're a fact of modern life. I think it's far better to put people on notice that they're doing a bit too much phone-checking during the meetings – and they will stop. So, I guess I'm putting Deborah on notice: She needs to watch the amount of time she's spending on her iPhone during the meetings."

- "My only advice to Deborah can be summed up in four words: Turn off your iPhone. I realize she is a sitting CFO, and she can't "go dark" on her own team for hours on end. But it's evident that she gets distracted by emails and texts during our board meetings – and she's such a good director that we want her full attention."

- "When the board meets, there is a row of chairs behind one side of the board table where members of management sit during the meetings. The people sitting there can all see the iPads of the board members sitting in front of them. And when they look at Deborah's iPad, they see that she is frequently checking the stock price of her own company and reading articles in the Wall Street Journal. In fairness, some peoples' presentations in our board meetings drone on and on – so, I really can't blame her. But she should try to limit that a bit."

- "Repeat after me: My name is Deborah and I have an iPhone problem."

Appendix C-1:

SAMPLE DIRECTOR EXPECTATIONS

THE FOLLOWING EXPECTATIONS of the Board of Directors were developed from interviews held in December 2017 with all ABC board members and members of ABC's management team who regularly interface with the board.

- **Preparation:** Prepare for board and committee meetings by reviewing the pre-reading materials in advance and reflecting on the key issues to be discussed. Come to the meetings ready to address the agenda items and get engaged in the discussions and debates.

- **Participation**: Actively participate in the board and committee meetings, drawing on your experience and expertise to bring relevant and constructive insights and perspectives into the board dialogue. Avoid dominating the board dialogue and/or speaking to "get your name in the minutes". Offer differing or contrary points of view where appropriate.

- **Attentive:** Remain attentive and conscientious throughout board and committee meetings, avoiding the temptation to be distracted by electronic devices, etc.

- **Integrity/Confidentiality:** Always act with integrity and ethics. Focus on the best interests of ABC and its shareholders in board decision-making. Respect the confidentiality of board discussions and ABC business issues.

- **Avoid Micro-Management**: Focus your questions and comments at a governance/oversight level.

- **Say It in the Meeting**: Express your views in the meeting, not after the meeting is over.

- **Mutual Respect**: Engage with management and fellow directors in a respectful manner even when making a counterpoint or expressing strong disagreement. Make an effort to build a constructive working relationship with fellow board members and members of the ABC management team.

- **Responsiveness:** Be responsive in replying to management requests and inquiries between meetings, wherever possible responding within 48 hours, even to acknowledge receipt of the request if it is not possible to attend to it within that timeframe.

- **Keep Current**: Make an ongoing effort to keep abreast of developments in [ABC's industry], the global economy, key markets in regions where ABC does business and developments in public company governance. Make an effort to listen in to ABC's earnings calls with the financial analysts.

Appendix C-2:

SAMPLE BOARD EXPECTATIONS OF MANAGEMENT

THE FOLLOWING EXPECTATIONS of the ABC Management Team in working with Board of Directors were developed from interviews held in December 2017 with all ABC board members and those members of ABC's management team who regularly interface with the board.

- **Leadership and Managerial Competence**: Run the company in a competent, businesslike way, providing leadership to the people who work at ABC to achieve strategic and financial goals.

- **Accountability**: Take responsibility for ABC's performance and the achievement of corporate objectives; follow through on commitments.

- **Integrity:** Operate with ethics and integrity in running the company and in dealings with the Board.

- **Preparation**: Put effort into the pre-reading materials in preparation for Board and Committee meetings so as to make the best use of the board's time. Focus on the key issues, provide not just data and information but your insights into what the data means and the alternatives you have considered in making your recommendations to the Board.

- **Provide Industry Context**: Provide the board with information that enables directors to compare ABC with competitors in [ABC's industry] in terms of financial performance and other key metrics.

- **Provide Strategic Linkage**: Highlight the linkage between management proposals and ABC's strategic direction and strategic goals in preparing board materials and presentations.

- **Avoid Micro-Management**: Focus your pre-reading materials, board presentations, and discussions at a governance level; try to avoid dragging the board into management details.

- **Transparency/Mutual Respect**: Be candid in sharing your thinking with the board and in seeking their views on issues where they can be a true strategic thought partner to management. Don't get defensive if a board member asks a tough question or challenges your thinking.

- **Don't Surprise the Board**: Let the board know about important issues which are emerging – both potential problems and "big wins" – in a timely fashion.

Appendix D

DIRECTOR EVALUATION PROCESS

Step	Description
Create and Distribute Interview Protocols	➤ I find it preferable to use a few general questions and probe for examples and specifics during the interviews. But I nonetheless recommend sending out the interview protocol in advance. This gets directors thinking about what they'll say relative to each of their colleagues, producing richer, more constructive feedback. ➤ One key question to consider: Will interviewees be asked whether their fellow board members should be re-nominated? This is not an essential question, and some boards feel uncomfortable about including it; but this issue should probably be discussed when the protocol is developed.
Interviews	➤ Zoom or other videoconferencing technology can be used for interviews to eliminate travel costs associated with in-person interviews and accelerate the project timeline. ➤ Typically, only board members (including the CEO) are interviewed in a director evaluation process. However, this practice may change over time. The New Director 360, discussed earlier, includes senior executives who regularly attend board and committee meetings as well as external advisors to the board (external auditors, compensation consultants, etc.)

Develop Individual Feedback Reports	➢ Interview feedback is analyzed and summarized. ➢ An individual feedback report is prepared for each director. ➢ Typically, draft reports are reviewed with the Board Chair before they are finalized; a summary of key findings may also be provided to the Nominating and Governance Committee if evaluations are going to be factored into director re-nomination decisions
Debrief/ Discussion	➢ The external facilitator meets/Zooms with each director individually to discuss their feedback. ➢ There is no need for an Action Plan. Individual director feedback reports should provide a level of specificity that enables recipients to understand any problems surfaced in the evaluation and discuss with the interviewer what steps they might take to address them.

About the Author

Beverly Behan has the greatest job in the world.

She's had the privilege of working with Boards of Directors of the S&P1500 and listed companies around the globe for the past twenty-five years – some of the smartest, nicest, most fascinating, and most accomplished people in the world, who keep her at the top of her game. Her clients are typically boards that want to get to the top of *their* game – and stay there.

To date, she's worked with nearly 200 boards, ranging from recent IPOs to the Fortune 500 – from New York and Toronto to Bogota, Kuala Lumpur, and Tel Aviv.

Beverly has interviewed thousands of directors in conducting board and director evaluations, dating back to 1996 when undertook the first director peer review for a major North American bank. In 2001, she incorporated management input into board evaluations for a Fortune 500 publishing company. In 2015, she conducted the first board and director evaluations for one of the largest conglomerates in Southeast Asia – overcoming the concern that individual director evaluations couldn't be effectively adapted to Asian business culture. Over the past decade, she's worked with a number of boards on the development of Board 2.0, an innovation to help boards optimize their composition and manage that transition effectively. And in 2019, she worked with the board of a Fortune 100 company to create what became the New Director 360. The insights she gained from this work, focusing on the effectiveness of boards and of individual directors, have been the foundation for *Becoming a Boardroom Star*.

Beverly is the author of *Great Companies Deserve Great Boards* (Palgrave MacMillan, 2011) named Governance Book of the Year by *Directors & Boards* magazine and ranked #1 for four weeks on the *Globe & Mail* business best seller list in Canada. During the COVID-19 lockdowns in 2021, Beverly authored *Board and Director Evaluations: Innovations for 21st Century Governance Committees* and *New CEOs and Boards: How to Build a Great Board Relationship – and a Great Board*, which are scheduled for release in the third and fourth quarters of 2021.

A former partner at Mercer Delta in New York and Global Managing Director of the Hay Group's Board Effectiveness practice, Beverly started her own firm, Board Advisor, LLC, in New York in 2009. She can be reached at Beverly.behan@boardadvisor.net.

Why I Started Working with Boards of Directors

About 30 years ago, I took a job with a major Canadian airline – one that no longer exists. It was a prestigious company, and its board was populated by marquee-name directors. But it faced major challenges during the First Gulf War – oil prices had skyrocketed, and people were afraid to travel. Canadian law did not afford our airline the protections of Chapter 11, which our US counterparts were invoking at the time.

To save the company, a group of employees initiated a "wages for stock" arrangement coupled with a joint venture with American Airlines, which needed better access to Asian airports. We managed to negotiate a deal with our unions that involved wage cuts of 5–20%, with these moneys invested in company stock. Morale was electric; people who worked for the airline took pride in their efforts to save it from bankruptcy. The deal raised something in the range of $750 million.

But things soured when the proxy circular revealed that the CEO's salary had been increased, largely offsetting his 20% salary cut. In response, the board sent a letter to the homes of company employees, attempting to justify the pay decision. This inflamed the situation and outraged the company's unions. A retired pilot admonished the board at the Annual Shareholder's Meeting – making national headlines. The CEO was replaced – by someone who had run a commercial real estate company in the same Calgary office tower as the airline's headquarters. Within the company, jokes circulated: "Our board members must have run into this guy in the elevator!" The downward spiral continued until the airline was sold to its major rival; tens of thousands lost their jobs. This was my first exposure to how the decisions made by a Board of Directors impacts the "tone at the top" of a company – and peoples' lives.

I left the airline shortly after the proxy fiasco and returned to private practice at a Vancouver law firm. There, I worked with other boards – nearly all of which were lackluster and characterized by a "country club" mentality. To me, the boardroom was supposed to be where the buck stopped – where smart, capable, experienced people called the question and made a difference. But I saw none of that.

About that time, a Canadian report entitled "*Where Were the Directors?*" was issued by the Toronto Stock Exchange. It was a scathing rebuke of the dismal state of corporate governance in Canada.

I read it on a Vancouver beach as if it were a racy novel. It confirmed many of the disturbing things I had begun to realize about the way most boards were functioning at that time.

As I flipped the pages – almost breathlessly – my friends asked, "What on earth are you reading?" "I'm reading this corporate governance thing!" "Bev," they told me, "you've gotta get a life!"

And I realized they were right. I knew in that moment what I wanted to do: I wanted to work with Boards of Directors – to try to make those boards all that they should be.

A few months later, I joined the executive compensation practice of Wm Mercer. I wasn't terribly interested in compensation. I was interested in working in the boardroom day in and day out – looking for opportunities to focus on board effectiveness issues.

I didn't have long to wait: One of the largest banks in Canada had a shareholder activist and I was brought in to provide advice. This led to conducting the bank's board evaluation, which included an individual director evaluation – one of the first ever undertaken by the board of a major North American company.

I was then transferred to New York, where I became a partner in the corporate governance practice of Mercer Delta. Enron fell – and suddenly board effectiveness became the hottest topic in corporate America. I've now had the privilege of working with boards around the world for 25 years. And my view has never changed. I believe that great companies deserve great boards – and great boards require great directors.

Endnotes

Chapter 1

1 PwC, "Turning Crisis Into Opportunity," *Annual Corporate Directors Survey* (October 2020), 15. Accessed October 18, 2020, www.pwc.com/us/en/services/governance-insights-center/assets/pwc-2020-annual-corporate-directors-survey.pdf.

2 PwC, "The collegiality conundrum: Finding balance in the boardroom," *Annual Corporate Directors Survey*, (October 2019). Accessed June 29, 2021, www.pwc.com/us/en/services/governance-insights-center/assets/pwc-2019-annual-corporate-directors-survey-full-report-v2.pdf.pdf.

3 PwC, "Insights from the Boardroom 2012," PwC's *Annual Corporate Directors Survey* (October, 2012), 8. Accessed June 29, 2021, www.pwc.com/us/en/corporate-governance/annual-corporate-directors-survey/assets/pdf/pwc-annual-corporate-directors-survey.pdf.

4 *Great Companies Deserve Great Boards* (Palgrave MacMillan, 2011) is a book I wrote ten years ago that was named 'Governance Book of the Year' by Directors & Boards magazine. I chose the title because it's something I strongly believe.

Chapter 3

5 Most of my work with boards involves board-building – taking a board from "good to great" and keeping a great board vibrant using comprehensive board and director evaluations among other tools. Readers with an interest in this topic may enjoy *Board and Director Evaluations: Innovations for 20th Century Governance Committees* (2021, Board Advisor, LLC) or my on-line workshop, Innovations in Board-Building. See www.boardadvisor.net – and use WORKSHOP25 for a 25% discount on the workshop price.

6 Jan Masaoka, "What is Micromanagement and What Isn't?" *Blue Avocado*, November 15, 2010, https://blueavocado.org/board-of-directors/what-is-micromanagement-and-what-isn-t/.

7 Conscious Governance, "Ending micromanagement around the Boardroom: A primer for Directors." Accessed June 29, 2021, https://consciousgovernance.com/blog-archives/ending-micromanagement-around-the-boardroom-a-primer-for-directors.

8 Ellis Carter, "How to Survive a Micro-Managing Board", *Charity Lawyer Blog*, September 19, 2016. Accessed June 29, 2021, https://charitylawyerblog.com/2016/09/19/how-to-survive-a-micro-managing-board.

9 Stuart Levine, "Are you Prepared for Your Next Board Meeting?" *Forbes*, August 28, 2016. Accessed June 29, 2021, www.forbes.com/sites/forbesinsights/2016/08/28/are-you-prepared-for-your-next-board-meeting/?sh=62b693eeaf71.

10 Spencer Stuart, 2020 U.S. *Spencer Stuart Board Index*, 22–23. Accessed June 29, 2021, https://www.spencerstuart.com/research-and-insight/us-board-index

11 Lansie Sylvia, "How Many Hours Should I Be Devoting to Non-Profit Board Service Every Month?" *Generocity*, June 29, 2016.

12 Natalie Cooper, Lamm, Bob, and Val Morrison, Randy, *Board Practices Report: Common threads across boardrooms* (New York: Society for Corporate Governance and Deloitte Development LLC, 2019), 11. Accessed June 29, 2021 www2.deloitte.com/us/en/pages/center-for-board-effectiveness/articles/us-board-practices-report-common-threads.html.

13 Jon Michail, "Strong Nonverbal Skills Matter Now More than Ever in this 'New Normal'," Forbes, August 24, 2020. Accessed June 29, 2021,www.forbes.com/sites/forbescoachescouncil/2020/08/24/strong-nonverbal-skills-matter-now-more-than-ever-in-this-new-normal/?sh=767bd0ac5c61; Adrian Dearnell, "It's Not What You Say, It's How You Say it", Forbes, July 10, 2018. Accessed June 29,2021, www.forbes.com/sites/adriandearnell/2018/07/10/its-not-what-you-say-its-how-you-say-it-why-perception-matters-when-

14 Jeff Thompson, "Is Nonverbal Communication a Numbers Game?" *Psychology Today*, September 30, 2011. Accessed June 29, 2021, www.psychologytoday.com/us/blog/beyond-words/201109/is-nonverbal-communication-numbers-game; Philip Yaffe, "The 7% rule – fact, fiction or misunderstanding," *Ubiquity*, Vol. 2011, Issue October. Accessed June 29, 2021, https://dl.acm.org/doi/10.1145/2043155.2043156; Nick Morgan, "Debunking the Debunkers – the Mehrabian Myth Explained (Correctly)," *Public Words*, July 23, 2009. Accessed June 29, 2021, https://dl.acm.org/doi/10.1145/2043155.2043156.

Chapter 13

15 If your board is working with a new CEO or about to undertake a CEO transition, you might find *New CEOs and Boards: How to Build a Great Board Relationship – and a Great Board*, 2021, Board Advisor, LLC to be helpful in this regard. See www.boardadvisor.net for details.

Chapter 14

16 PwC, "Turning Crisis Into Opportunity", *Annual Corporate Directors Survey*, (October 2020), 15. Accessed June 29, 2021, www.pwc.com/us/en/services/governance-insights-center/assets/pwc-2020-annual-corporate-directors-survey.pdf.

17 Ibid., 15.

18 Beverly Behan, *Board and Director Evaluations: Innovations for 21st Century Governance Committees* (Board Advisor, 2021).

19 For more information on Board 2.0, see www.boardadvisor.net, or see *Board and Director Evaluations, Innovations for 21st Century Governance Committees*, Board Advisor, 2021, or *"Board Evaluation: Building Board 2.0"*, The Corporate Board, January–February 2021.

20 UK Financial Reporting Council, *The UK Corporate Governance Code*, July 2018. Accessed June 29, 2021, www.frc.org.uk/getattachment/88bd8c45-50ea-4841-95b0-d2f4f48069a2/2018-UK-Corporate-Governance-Code-FINAL.pdf

BECOMING A BOARDROOM STAR: THE WORKSHOP

If you enjoyed the book, you might enjoy the author's on-line workshop, Becoming a Boardroom Star, now available worldwide.

It includes videos that correspond to every chapter

- Stars and Dogs
- Governance is a Team Sport
- Five Board Archetypes
- Drinking from a Firehose
- Site Visits
- Nose In, Fingers Out
- New Director 360s
- Boardrooms are Like Fishbowls
- 10 Common Boardroom Pitfalls
- Profiles in Boardroom Courage
- A Boardroom Star Becomes a Boardroom Champion
- Becoming a Board Committee Chair
- Key Facets of the Board Chair's Role
- Director Performance Management
- Prove Them Right!

You can learn more about the workshop at: www.boardadvisor.net.

Use coupon code Workshop25 at checkout for 25% off the workshop price, which takes the price from $199 to only $149 in the US, with similar reductions in other countries).

INDIVIDUAL WORKSHOPS FOR BOARDROOM CHAMPIONS

The New Boardroom Landscape: This workshop focuses on the underpinnings of board effectiveness, the transitions most boards made over the past two decades, five board archetypes that characterize most boards today (and which one best describes your board) and the necessary pre-requisites to make the shift nearly every board worldwide now wants to achieve.

Board Leadership – Hallmarks of a Boardroom Champion: What sets board champions apart when it comes to board facilitation, working relationship with the Chief Executive Officer and keeping a "finger on the pulse" of the board? We'll discuss the importance of well-considered "board choreography" in leading tough decisions in the boardroom and the key role of the Chair/Lead Director in both board and director effectiveness – including tools to help you optimize both.

Optimizing Board Composition – from Board 2.0 to Director Orientation: This workshop takes a comprehensive and forward-looking approach to the issue of board composition, including a working session on designing Board 2.0 for your own board. It covers the use of director expectations, director recruitment packages, strategies to optimize diversity recruitment objectives and upgrading your director orientation program, including the New Director 360, a 2019 innovation from a F100 client.

CEO Succession Planning – the Board's Most Critical Decision: The most important decision any board will make is nearly always their choice of Chief Executive Officer. That's why the board needs to be firmly in the driver's seat on CEO succession planning – orchestrating a comprehensive CEO succession plan that incorporates insights from every member of the board and the sitting CEO. We'll introduce the CEO succession roadmap – and two critical steps your board needs to take before calling a headhunter.

Board Evaluation – The Biggest Secret in Creating a Great Board: Most board evaluations are a squandered opportunity. But redesigned, board evaluations can become a watershed exercise that takes your board "from good to great". We'll outline what's required to make this shift –including the use of structured, Zoom based interviews rather than surveys –whether (and how) to incorporate management feedback and a range of other issues. And we'll answer practical questions about pros/cons of introducing these new elements to your current board evaluation process.

Director Performance Management – Stepping up to the Most Awkward Issue Many Board Leaders Face: This workshop focuses on four Director Performance Management Tools every board champion should know about. We'll discuss the importance of tailoring your approach to the performance issue at hand – behavioral issues vs expertise issues. The session will be designed to include plenty of time to confidentially discuss any director performance issues currently on your mind. We sign Confidentiality Agreements in advance.

Individual Workshop Format:

These are designed as 90-minute individual, one-on-one workshops to enable you to have an entirely open, confidential discussion about your own board in the context of the workshop topic. For more information, email Beverly.behan@boardadvisor.net. Each workshop includes:

- ✓ A 15-minute pre-workshop Zoom/call to clarify your objectives; this ensures that the 90-minute session is focused accordingly;

- ✓ Confidentiality Agreement signed by Board Advisor prior to each session to ensure that discussion during the workshop can be open and candid;

- ✓ eCopy of our *Board-Building Toolkit*

Workshops for Your Entire Board?

If you're interested in arranging a workshop for your entire board or a board committee on any of these topics, feel free to get in touch! We can accommodate these via videoconference or in person, depending on your location.

Other Books for Your Governance Library

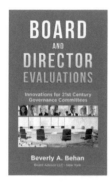  

Join Our Mailing List

It's free to sign up. Just visit our website at www.boardadvisor.net.

 We'll keep you up to date about book launches, workshops, discounts, complimentary articles, and other items of interest. And don't worry about "email overkill" – we know how annoying that can be. You'll only hear from us when we have something we think will interest you.

While you're there, check out the Board Advisor Mailbag and our latest free digital downloads. A recent visitor called our website "a corporate governance wonderland."

Made in United States
Troutdale, OR
10/25/2023